POEMS AND MORE

The Stories of Lives Well Lived

Edna Holmes

MaxHoltMedia

© 2015 **Edna Holmes**

Published by MaxHoltMedia
303 Cascabel Place, Mount Juliet, TN 37122
www.maxholtmedia.com

Scriptures quoted are from the King James Version of the Bible

Cover design by: Max Holt Media
Cover Photos enhanced by Eddie Holt

ISBN-13: 978-1-944537-03-6

CONTENTS

ACKNOWLEDGEMENTS

Much thanks and appreciation goes to my husband for his patience and endurance as I launched out again into the 'sea of writing'. He has been my mainstay for sixty-four years of marriage.

Several good friends have encouraged me through the years about my poetry. But Neecie, my sister, was my "sounding board". She heard it first, and approved of every single piece I wrote with such enthusiasm I felt like a poet...of sorts, and was greatly encouraged to continue writing.

My brother, Max, has given me the opportunity to expand and revise this poem book and have it republished with a different title and cover. I'm grateful for that, and his willingness to guide me along that path.

My brothers and sisters have given me permission to quote from their writings in our Family Memories, and other sources where I may glean additional information about our family history. It has made the family poems more meaningful. I'm very thankful for their sharing.

My son, Louis, helps me set up for each writing project on the computer. Otherwise, I'd likely be pounding the old typewriter. He and Jan are patient helpers as I need them. I'm grateful for their 'being there' for me.

DEDICATION

In Memory Of
William Bruce Holt

November 25, 1950 - December 21, 2011

Bruce is the youngest of seven brothers and three sisters. All of us born of the same parents, we have retained a closeness through decades even though we have been scattered far and wide and only come together every year to our family reunion. Our baby brother was the last to join us in life, and the first to leave us in death. We grieve; but because his hope was in Christ, we know we will see him again in heaven.

PARENTS

William Kelly Holt
March 23, 1902 – November 24. 1979

Willie Louise Holt
December 25, 1907 - May 16, 1988

FOREWORD

These poems were originally shared with only family and friends. Eventually they were published. This book is the expansion and revision of the first one. Most poems I've written are included plus many notes and personal writings of my brothers and sisters in the family section. I'm grateful for the permission to use this rich material in the book.

The Family poems are touched with humor and are typical of country families of that era when folks lived off the farm and life was simple. They depict life as it generally was in our big growing family. Most are merely little stories strung together in verse form. The related memories of my siblings when growing up make the poems much more meaningful.

Memories to Keep holds more memories of my brothers and sisters from the Family Memories book. They furnish so much detail of our family life *back then*. They are invaluable.

Miscellaneous poems are the collection of "bits and pieces of lasting impressions" written through the years.

Poems that 'sprang' from Bible verses evolved during the four decades I served as a pastor's wife. Several have already been published in the daily Bible devotional book, *Treasures to Keep.*

The Child poems have been most beneficial, and have earned their place. I couldn't leave them behind.

Grandma Bit is my afterthought to encourage grandmothers to make the most of their grandmother roles. You will see in these little verses and writings a doting grandmother's love and delight in her grandchildren and also *great* grandchildren. I encourage you to learn new and special ways to shower love on your children's children.

PART I

Family Poems

*A Collection of
Memories
In Verse*

This family picture, taken in 2010, was the last one taken of the ten Holt children together before our brother Bruce died. The birth order is right to left from our oldest sister seated on the end of the first row and ending with the youngest (Bruce) standing behind her.

"And Neecie, Willie, Edna, Jack,

Dan, John, Frank, Mack,

Connie and Bruce came along....

If Mama and Daddy didn't have
so many kids...

I couldn't sing this song!"

From: *The Holt Family Song*
By: Max Holt

EDNA HOLMES

1 - THE FAMILY

Poems--Comments--Stories—Quotes

OUR FAMILY'S BEGINNING

Our Father's and Mother's lives together began in 1925. On their 50th Wedding Anniversary in 1975, Mama wrote down what she could remember of the details of their wedding day. I am quoting the story, exactly as she wrote it.

"Yes, fifty years ago today, I was the happiest girl in Texas. I was marrying the most handsome man in the country. He was a real man too...6 ft. 2 inches and weighed 184 pounds. Had a wealth of auburn hair and the cutest ways I ever saw.

We got married on Wednesday, April 8, 1925 at the courthouse in Clarksville, Texas. Your Daddy had on a charcoal colored suit with speckled red and gray thread in it. Also a white shirt and tie with new tan oxfords. I had on a light pink taffeta dress with a white bow in front and lace around the collar. Short sleeved. We were married about 11:30 in the morning, then went out and had lunch. Momma (Sadie) had come with us, and she did some shopping before we left Clarksville and headed back home. Papa and Momma lived on the *Old Man Wooley Place* on Red River, about 2 miles further past the Bailey Farm.

We spent the first night there, and then moved to our own house the next day. It was a lovely old-fashioned house with climbing roses and honeysuckle vines all over the place. My whole family loved Bill, and every Saturday night we went to Papa's house. My step-mother was a good cook, and Bill loved good cooking." (End of quote)

Note: With that happy beginning our parents started a long and fruitful life together spanning the depression years, dust bowl days, and hard times as so many families suffered in that era. Their first child was born in 1927 and the last one in 1950, so Daddy and Mama's offspring overlap two generations. It is evident too, as the first four of us are referred to as *the older ones*, while the other six are *the younger ones*.

My oldest brother, Willie, told us of a vague memory he has of Mama and Daddy waltzing together when he was very young. "The music was playing and they were waltzing together around the room. The music had stopped, but they kept waltzing into a corner..."

With that snippet of a memory he had of our parents' younger years, I wrote a poem: *They Waltzed on Together.* My brother Max set the poem to music and has sung it for the family.

THEY WALTZED ON TOGETHER

She was just a country girl, pretty and shy
Who knew she'd been noticed and caught the eye
Of the rugged young farmer at the party that night
Playing his fiddle for the folks to dance by.

She lingered nearby as the next round started
Of a beautiful waltz, a favorite one;
Then he quietly laid his fiddle aside
And made his way to her, while music played on.

He extended his work hardened hand to hers
With a tender look she could see;
"You're the prettiest girl ever I've seen,
Would you dance this waltz with me?"

So they waltzed together; she was light as a feather
In strong arms that would hold her forever after;
The music stopped playing; they just kept waltzing
Into a corner and into a life.

After a long life, their music stopped playing;
They'd waltzed together, and left a rich legacy.
That special moment in our history,
Is when Daddy asked Mama:
"Will you waltz with me?"

Note: In remembering Daddy's hats, his work-worn old hat and his *go to town* hat, this poem came to mind one day. Now, it seems like a song with the first verse being the chorus; and a tune keeps playing around in my head, though I haven't been able to *capture* it for keeping with the words.

WATCHING DADDY'S HAT

He was a country gentleman
Though he laid no claim to that,
But we learned a heap of manners
Just by watching Daddy's hat.

He'd tip his hat politely if a lady he did meet
On the street, or just anywhere about.
It was a practice that we never would forget,
We saw it often watching Daddy's hat.

He had a certain nail to hang his good hat on,
And one for his working hat as well.
He took special care of his valuables like that,
And we learned too by watching Daddy's hat.

We minded our manners at the dinner table,
And were quiet while Daddy said grace.
He'd remove his hat at every meal;
It still is a gentleman's way.

So we grew up watching Daddy's hat;
His way was common, manly courtesy.
He didn't talk much about things like that;
We learned just by watching Daddy's hat.

A WORKING MAN

Note: In my growing up years I don't remember Daddy ever sleeping past daylight. He went early to the barn to feed the livestock and milk the cows. I wondered if he woke them up, too, like he did the family. He loved working the soil but also, coupled with farming, he had many other talents. He was an expert carpenter and builder. In any work he encouraged diligence in those working with him and for him. In addition, Daddy was a *country fiddler* who could entertain so well with his talent and personable manner. Both of our parents had musical talent that they passed along to their children; all ten of us have musical ability that has enriched our lives.

Our father had compassion for other people, especially *down and out* kinfolks who came around for help. Daddy always took them in, though we had a full house already. One incident which shows our father's character so well was related by Neecie, the oldest, who remembers things happening before the younger ones were born. She wrote in our family memories book:

Neecie: "About this time after the goat incident, Uncle Johnny left our place. Later, when we lived at Blakney, TX he came again to our house. He was sick and Daddy took care of him till he died. Mama and Daddy let him sleep in the living room where the best bed and fireplace were. When he died, Daddy made his coffin and bought some black cretonne and he carefully pleated and tacked each fold inside the coffin. I remember his big scarred hands (from picking cotton) working on the cloth. Daddy sent for the preacher, and had a funeral at the cemetery. We had a model A and Daddy drove home fast and I saw him wipe his eyes. So I thought to myself, *'He misses Uncle Johnny.'*"

Note: My fondest memories of Daddy were during the time we lived on the West Texas farm, the times he spent with the family sitting on the porch in late evening, after the day's work was done in the fields. He would tell us stories of his childhood. Sometimes, I'd get the guitar and strum along while we sang old songs our parents had taught us.

Later, one of us would get a pan of water and towel for Daddy to wash his feet before he went to bed. I know now what a soothing thing that must have been for his tired feet, for he seldom sat down during the day. He was a working man.

MEMORIES OF DADDY
(With Neecie and Willie)

Our Dad had many good sayings
To help us in learning and knowing;
The one at the top of my list of collection
Would be, "Tell it a-going."

Sister and Brother would lag behind
Hoeing cotton and corn in the season.
Happy children sharing fanciful dreams,
Until they'd hear "Tell it a-going!"

Now Daddy knew that dreams are special
And are difficult when working a hoe.
But it's important in life to work as you dream,
And tell it a-going as you go.

Often indecision grips me in this life,
And I sit for days just wondering...
Till a familiar, firm exhortation comes back:
"Get up, and tell it a-going!"

A LADY, ONE OF A KIND

Note: The most familiar memory I have of Mama is of her sitting and reading a book. Our mother loved to read, was a very avid reader, and read every book she could get her hands on. That gave her a wide range of knowledge. One of my brothers, when he began taking flying lessons, was amazed about how much Mama knew about the history of aviation.

By example, she influenced all her children to love reading. Late in her life, Mama had surgery done and most of her ten children were present. We were all gathered in the waiting room when a friend came in to sit with us. She said, *"I knew who the Holts were right away. All had something in front of their faces reading!"*

Mama could tell the most interesting facts and stories which was our entertainment at times. She had a vivid memory of details from books she read, and such perfect recall of the few movies (then called *shows*) she had seen, she could tell the stories so interestingly to us, we could almost see it on a screen.

But something she could never do well was to drive a car, especially a Model T! The peculiar way the gas was fed to the engine as the foot worked the clutch was a challenge at best. But she tried. Even though this was in the late 1930's, Daddy had acquired a brand new Model T Ford! Willie tells of the transaction in the Family Memories book:

Willie: "Once, Daddy did some work for an old farmer who had bought a new Model T Ford. Him and his wife did not like it. I think they were afraid of it, so they had set it in the barn and left it alone. Dad asked for the car for payment for his work. They were glad to get rid of it, so we had a new car. It would run really good and would start instantly."

Mama had an adventuresome spirit about her and she often surprised us with the sudden notion she'd get to do

23

something different. And so it was the day she decided to take what we called *dinner* out to Daddy and the older siblings at noon. I think he would have been most surprised if Mama had made it to the field in the car.

MEMORIES OF MAMA

Once when I was a little girl
In summer days following May,
My mother got the delightful notion
Of going to the field one day.

"We'll take a basket of food to eat
And surprise your daddy today"
'Twas like her to think of a picnic
At the end of the row in the shade.

We all climbed into the Model T car,
The top down, "How exciting!" we said,
And squealed with glee at the funny sight
Of Mama's hat brim flopping on her head.

For she tried and tried to the work the clutch
And feed gas at the same time.
For most that transaction wasn't much,
But Mama was a lady...one of a kind.

We clung with delight and watched Mama's hat flop
As the car circled in leaps so broad!
It was the greatest ride we ever had,
And never left the yard.

SISTER LEARNING TO DRIVE
(Neecie)

Daddy wasn't impressed with machinery;
He'd trade for the cheapest thing,
Especially a car in memorable days
When Sister first started driving.

It was humbling to drive a Model T car
Outdated as Noah's ark.
But Sister was determined to learn;
With the top down, she was off with a 'jerk'.

She headed down a woodsy road
Where no one could see or bother.
The country folk laughed at the sight
Of our car...it was like no other.

Sister was rolling along quite well
With confidence remembering each rule,
When suddenly, ahead in the middle of the road,
Was our elderly neighbor driving his mules!

The only thing she could think to do
Was hold to the wheel she was holding to.
The way to stop there was no one to say;
She stood up and screamed "GET OUT OF THE WAY!"

The old man scrambled with amazing speed
Himself and his mules to the side,
Then gazed in terrified wonder
As Sister sat down and continued her ride.

We are sure he told it at supper
And many times after to be,
Of the day he nearly met his Maker
Because of Sister in our old Model T.

MEMORIES OF OLE BUCK
(Willie)

When Daddy left the place one fall
For boll-pulling in the West,
He left big Brother in charge at home
As the substitute man of the house.

Now Brother usually started slow
With his chores around the place.
With Daddy's charge the picture changed:
Brother kept things done apace!

The key word was 'responsible'...
That's what Daddy had said.
Brother remembered that seriously,
Then Mama got this notion in her head.

It was the big election time;
Mama determined to go vote.
"I'll take ole Buck...he will do fine."
Brother's heart jumped up his throat!

Buck was his own, a spirited horse;
Nobody else ever rode him!
If anything happened to Mama...
To face Daddy, he couldn't imagine.

Mama's mind was set, it was final.
"I rode horses before you were born!"
So she rebuked him for doubting;
Brother gloomily led Buck from the barn.

He guided the horse right to the porch,
Where Mama waited in riding regalia.
'This can't be happening' thought Brother,
As Mama stepped from porch to saddle.

Brother held his breath, waiting for Buck
To throw Mama off his back.
Instead he trotted off up the road,
A picture we'd never forget.

Mama's full skirt flowed behind,
For covering and color no lack,
And ole Buck acted like a pussycat
All the way there...and back!

Then we understood horse sense;
Ole Buck displayed it his way.
He too would have had to face Daddy...
If he had throwed Mama that day.

Note: Mama had truly ridden horses *before we were born.* As a young girl she grew up working in the fields and also doing house work and chores for her step-mother, Sadie, who had married her father when Mama was ten years old. Sadie could not read or write, which was not so uncommon in the early 1900's. In a certain time period, Sadie was selling butter to the sawmill workers for their families. She would send Mama by horseback to deliver the butter and take care of the business of the sale.

Note: It seems that Mama and Daddy spaced their off-spring by pairs. We had our *buddies* with which (because of close age) we naturally experienced more together:

Neecie and Willie, Edna and Jack, Dan and John, Frank and Max, and Connie and Bruce.

I have more actual experience to write about with the *older ones* for I was in that time slot. The stories related to me by my siblings in later years are the basis for some of the poems about *the younger ones*. It would take a large book to hold all the adventures that our family experienced living on a farm in the era before modernization of the rural areas began to change our world and times into a more complex way of life.

PENNY-SUCKERS
(Edna and Jack)

Saturdays were very special
When Daddy would go into town,
And bring Brother and me penny-suckers;
Then we'd run and let the well bucket down

And pull up that cool clear water,
At our age no small feat.
We'd dunk our suckers, then lick real slow;
Only a heathen would crunch one with his teeth.

We passed the hour in childish pleasure,
Savoring right down to the stick.
Never was so much for a penny;
There must have been a zillion licks!

It seems like a lifetime has passed us,
Since Brother and I sat on the well
Enjoying our penny-suckers,
Not knowing how rich we were.

SUMMERTIME MEMORIES
(Edna)

The exciting thing in summer for me,
As a child on the Little's Place,
Was the fresh-hay bumblebee buzzing time
And me with a board ready for the race!

The bees would buzz our barn hallway,
Around hay in each loft stacked.
I'd chase them, jumping, swinging my board
Until hitting one with a resounding *whack*!

I got very skilled with my aiming;
'Twas a delightful pleasure for me
Batting the board in the direction
To connect for a *splat* with a bee.

Finally one dived between board and me;
I didn't know they could be so sly.
But figuring I'd *whack* till the last one,
He stung me good...right under the eye!

That sent me to the house hollering,
Like I was dying sure enough.
It wasn't me but my eye in danger,
For Mama generously dabbed it with snuff.

Moaning the loss of that eyesight
I sighed, squinting my good eye to see,
And thought as I gloomily watched them buzz:
I'd never *whack* another bumblebee.

Note: On the *Little's Place*, we didn't have a fireplace. The big metal drum stove Daddy made was the focal point in winter time.

At Christmas, I remember that the dishpans of fruits and candies that they put out for us to find on Christmas morning were placed near the stove. Daddy got whatever was needed for the family. If he couldn't buy or trade for it, he made it himself.

FETCHING FIREWOOD
(Neecie, Willie, Edna, Jack)

When fall winds began to stir
That certain chill in the air,
Daddy marked a day for cutting
And hauling firewood for winter care.

He'd choose a tree in woods nearby,
Cut down and chop limbs to size.
We strung out like ants working,
Fetching wood for a good supply.

Our stove gobbled wood greedily,
In no time using a stack.
It burned us on the front side,
And froze us in the back!

It was uniquely homemade
From a big round metal drum.
Daddy himself designed the thing;
There was no likely comparison

So that ample supply of firewood
Kept us half alive at the best:
Our front side warm and thriving,
And the back side froze to death!

TRAINING MAMA'S DUCKS
(Edna and Jack)

It didn't take long for Brother and me
To get Mama's ducks trained right.
We tirelessly trotted them from pond to barn,
Into position...water in sight.

The gentle slope from the barnyard
To the pond down in the pasture,
Made a perfect distance for ducks to fly,
That rarely did, except for our muster!

We shooed them, coaxed, lining them up,
Then shrieked and hollered a fright!
They'd take to flight, spreading their wings;
It was our childish delight.

They'd glide to the pool, skim over the water,
Then settle down and swim for shore.
We'd run through the pasture to the pond
Trotting them back for another show.

The memory is fresh as yesterday,
Watching that graceful flight.
Mama's ducks couldn't have done it,
If we hadn't trained them right.

BLACKBERRY PICKING
(Neecie, Willie, Edna , Jack)

On a certain day for picking blackberries,
Mama managed to drive the car
Up the road to the best place of harvest,
With the kids, buckets, dishpans, and jars.

We filled everything up with berries,
Sure that winter would find us content
With plenty of berry jelly and jam;
We set off for the house...plum spent.

As soon as Mama got the car rolling,
Brother curiously looked at the gage,
And told Mama excitedly "HURRY!"
Or we will run out of gas on the way.

Mama, taking Brother's sage advice,
Took off like a shot from a gun!
We hung onto buckets and dishpans
As we made that desperate run.

We all saw the sapling across the road
In the place where nothing should be;
Mama gripped the wheel and tightened her lip
And bucked the car right over that tree!

The containers of blackberries
Took to flight, and in mid-air
Turned upside down in graceful rolls,
Dumping blackberries everywhere.

The back seat filled up, running over,
Up to our elbows and chins;
Mama never slowed, kept her eye on the road,
Determined to win...and she did!

Since growing up I've driven for miles,
Enough to circle the world.
I don't recollect very many of them,
But remember every mile that Mama drove!

Note: Not only did Mama cause a stir when she attempted to drive the car, the siblings as well were constantly trying to learn as young people naturally do. The empty roads with no traffic made it ideal to practice driving. Oftentimes it created a very memorable experience.

PEA-PICKING
(Willie and Neecie)

Fall pea-picking time had arrived;
Folks invited neighbors to gather,
Sharing bounty from each others' fields.
Daddy sent Sister and Brother.

He had traded the family car
For a pick-up long past it's prime.
Brother was convinced he could drive it;
In the country, Daddy didn't mind.

Brother could handle it very well,
His feet barely touching the floor.
But Sister was always uneasy:
He drove fast...as it would go!

They reached the pea patch up the road,
And were to go in and shut the gap.
Brother couldn't stop when he got there;
He went through it, ripping it out!

(Continued)

The brakes had failed and with quick speed
And the wire gate hung on the hood;
Brother franticly spied a lone pear tree
And stopped the pickup with a "THUD!"

Pears rained down like a hailstorm
On the cab and pickup back.
They scrambled out and replaced the gap
In the fence before the cows got out.

They hurried to pick their lot of peas,
And left there eager for home
To relate their tale of misfortune.
Daddy tried to look stern...

"I can't even turn my back,
But you kids get into some mischief!"
Meekly, Brother and Sister agreed.
Then each munched a pear from the lone pear tree.

Note: Being the oldest, it was Neecie and Willie's lot to work in the fields together during the seasons. The friendship they developed as children has lasted all their lives. Neecie writes about adjusting to sharing the attention when Willie was born.

Neecie: "I was 2 years and 1 month old when Willie was born. I had been spoilt and coddled so I must have been jealous of the attention Willie got. Mama said she was in the kitchen and heard Willie cry out and she came in and found me on the bed with him. There was a red spot on his arm. She said *'Did you pinch the baby?'* I said 'He hit me first!' He was 3 months old."

Note: It has been known that people have remembered things at a very early age, and I have such a memory, though a very small snippet, of a very big, important happening. Not quite three years old, I remember a large crowd of black folk gathered around our house veranda and in the yard listening to Daddy's radio as he had invited them to come hear the boxing match when Joe Louis of boxing fame became the world heavy-weight champion. The noise of it all and their excitement imprinted that memory in me. Strangely, I did not realize the memory was about an important historical event in history until I'd written the poem and looked up the information.

EARLY MEMORY
(Edna)

It is a rare recollection,
Surprising for one so young.
But it's a treasure of remembrance
Of Daddy's kindness and concern.

The big event would be broadcast
On the country's radios.
Hardly any folks in our parts had one,
But our Dad, who would share with all.

So the black folks came from far and near;
Our yard and porch were full.
It was their champion making his bid;
The evening would not be dull!

Daddy sat out on the porch
Together with all his friends,
Tuned the radio in to the fight,
And settled down for that special evening.

(Continued)

I remember the whoops and hollers
Which were triggered every minute or so.
I was leaning on Daddy's big shoulder,
Thoroughly enjoying the 'show'.

When that excited crowd applauded,
I'd jump up and down with glee,
Swinging on Daddy's overall straps;
It's easy to do when you are three!

That's all that I remember
Of that scene so long ago.
I know Daddy gave so much pleasure
By kindly sharing his radio.

Note: It was during that period of time that the most unforgettable character of my childhood came into focus. My favorite in the Family Poems is about Dicey, the Midwife. Beginning with Jack, born when I was two years old, Dicey delivered three more of my brothers before Daddy moved our family to West Texas.

A black lady, Dicey was the most respected and revered person in our community because she brought all the babies! Nobody was more important, but I did not like her because she only brought us boys! I was very sure that she brought them in that little black bag she carried. In my little child mind, the only way babies could have gotten into the house was in Dicey's black bag.

Each time she came and left again, we had another one! All the community children seemed to be hers; they gathered around her when she came about and she patted them on their heads calling them *her chullun*. I was relieved that I was not born there, so was not one of Dicey's *chullun*. If she had brought us a baby girl just once I would have loved her! But it didn't happen. The house was filling up with boys, and she kept bringing them!

DICEY THE MIDWIFE
(Through the eyes of a child)

She was the most special lady
The country folk had ever got;
She was their angel of mercy,
As black as Mama's wash pot.

Her value lay in folks' desperate need
To keep the population a-going;
Dicey brought babies for miles around,
Because she was the one with the knowing.

(Continued)

She hatched out all the brand new ones,
In some way got the right tags,
And after sorting and deciding on the time,
Delivered them in her little black bag.

I dreaded her ample form coming;
We got far more than our share.
Daddy couldn't do a thing about Dicey,
Yet he could easily whop a bear!

She took advantage of kindness,
And killed out all my joy;
For each time she came to our house,
She'd leave us another boy.

She loved to pet her 'chullun',
When appearing around where they'd be.
But not one pat did she lay on my head;
I kept distance between her...and me.

For I *knew* where I came from;
Sister and Brother told me...in a way.
It was thrilling each time I heard it;
I didn't come in Dicey's black bag!

My folks found me on the creek bank,
About to roll into the water.
They were tickled as can be,
Saying "Here's us a baby daughter."

Now Dicey often looked at me kindly,
Like she knew something I didn't.
It made no difference; I'd forever brag:
Dicey didn't bring *me* in her little black bag.

Note: In this same place, when I was five years old, the worst trauma of my young life occurred. My brother and I were out getting in firewood for the cook stove in the kitchen. It was late in the evening but Daddy was not yet home from the field. I was squatted down stacking wood in my arms to carry in as Willie swung the ax to secure it in the chopping block. It glanced off and came around hitting me in the temple of the left side of my head.

He quickly slapped his hands on each side of my head and walked me to the back door where Mama took action as country women had to do in those days! She dumped sugar on a towel, poured coal oil on that and wrapped it tightly around my head. (I've related that to doctors in this era, and they are incredulous!)

However, country folks living far away from a doctor had to do something when such accidents happened in the family. I don't remember feeling anything; I was not afraid until my father stepped through the back door and I saw the fear in his eyes. I started muttering the only *cuss word* I knew at the time:

Golly, my Golly....my golly...my golly....

Daddy did not allow us to say words like that. He said it was "*too near to cuss words.*" But he let me sit there on Mama's lap with my head swathed in a towel...and cuss! Then they laid me in their bed in the room with the fireplace. Daddy said Santa Claus had come early and brought me a big doll. He fetched it from the smokehouse where they had hidden our Christmas toys.

Perhaps my parents were afraid that I might die. Though Mama must have been terrified at the sight of me already drenched in blood as my brother brought me in, she acted quickly, saving my life. I do not remember it, but later they did take me to a doctor in town. At that time, and many others in my lifetime, I know that God spared my life because He had a purpose for me living.

A MEMORY OF TRAUMA
(Willie, Edna in Dec. 1939)

The sun was near to setting
As Brother worked at the chore
Of cutting the supply of firewood
For our kitchen cook stove.

Little Sister nearby helping,
The shadow constantly around,
Sometimes where she shouldn't be...
She stooped now to the ground

And stacked cut wood in her arms
As Brother completed the chopping.
He aimed the axe to secure it
In the stump until the next using.

Instead, the axe glanced off the edge
Swinging wide in a fearful moment
Striking Sister in the temple...
It happened in an instant!

Brother, stunned by the frightful sight,
Slapped his hands to her head on the sides,
And half carried, half walked her to the door
Full of panic...he feared for her life.

Mama rushed to do what could be done,
Fetched a towel, coal oil and sugar...
She fixed it quickly wrapping Sister's head
With a prayer and hope for tomorrow.

Sister could sense the fear and fright
As Daddy hurriedly came from the field.
The look on his face was easily read...
She knew the danger was real.

Some words were not allowed to be said;
Repeating them would be folly.
She threw caution to the wind and muttered
My golly...my golly...my golly...

We all survived that awful time
And little Sister realized that day,
If folks were fearful that you might die,
You can say anything you want to say.

AFTERMATH OF TRAUMA
(December of 1939)

After that fearful hour was passed,
With her head bandaged huge in a ball,
They put little Sister to bed;
The fireplace flickered shadows on the wall.

Daddy had said since Christmas was near,
And Santa considered the occasion,
He sent a big doll on ahead,
The accident being a good reason.

From hiding the big baby doll was fetched
And was laid beside her on the bed.
It was near as big as Sister,
Who was trying to sort things in her head.

No one had seen Santa...the real one,
Or ever seen reindeer fly.
Nothing with four legs on the place
Had ever took to the sky!

(Continued)

When did Santa stop by here
Hiding a doll in the smokehouse outside?
Did Santa, whoever he was,
Know that she most nearly died?

The shadows flickered low on the wall
Lulling little Sister to sleep,
Weighted by the day's experience
And vivid memories she would keep.

Note: This was the period of time when more of our everyday life began to lodge in my memory. When we had moved to that community the little church house had been abandoned and someone had stacked hay inside of it. Daddy had protested to the land owner, and he gave permission to make it suitable for having church in it again.

Our Dad did that and made arrangements for having Sunday School for the children of the community. He also secured a preacher from town to come out occasionally for a Sunday service. On the Sundays with no preacher, the folks would just sing some hymns after Sunday School but there was no one who could play the old pump organ.

Daddy could play enough chords for people to sing by and I remember watching his huge (to me) hands move over the organ keys which were just level with my eyes. I was fascinated by the beautiful sounds that came from under Daddy's hands.

Note: Jack was the first one that Dicey, the midwife, brought to us in Blakney. At two years of age, I don't remember the event, but he was my closest sibling, and we had many adventures together as we grew up. Our memories may have a little different view as each one had his individual impression of things at the time. That is interesting to me as I've read our Family Memories book. Though Jack was only about four years old when we moved to The Little's place from there, he remembered vivid details which I don't recall at all about the process.

Jack's Memories: "I remember that Willie walked and led the cow. Everything was loaded in our wagon and Edna and I played on the coupling pole that stuck out the back. We would ride awhile and then jump off and run around the wagon then get back on the coupling pole."

Note: Being out and about with Daddy a lot, Jack had many sights and sounds experienced which made a permanent memory for him.

Jack: "One year, snakes got real bad in the Jackson slew, near where we lived. Everyone in the community donated a couple of hogs to eat the snakes. I remember riding in the wagon and Daddy wouldn't let me out. They turned the hogs loose and they did get after the snakes. That could have been when and where the wild hogs got started in Red River County. Charles Jackson still owns that property and a few months ago he mentioned that he remembered that also. He is about my age."

Note: Jack also remembers that fateful day when the Japanese bombed Pearl Harbor December 7, 1941. We had company with the adults sitting in the yard visiting on a Sunday afternoon.

Jack: "....Neecie came out on the porch crying and said that the Japanese had bombed Pearl Harbor. Daddy pulled his watch out of his overall bib and looked at it. The next day almost every man went to town to try and join the army to go *whoop'em.*"

Note: Before the family had moved from the Blakney to the Little's Place, our brother Dan was born. Dicey brought us another baby boy! My older sister and brother remember the occasion of Dicey coming to the house to take care of Mama that day. These were hard times for everyone. Money was hard to come by, but Daddy always managed to have money to pay Dicey the fee for her services.

Neecie: "Willie and I sat there at the table with Daddy (Dicey was still there) while Daddy opened his wallet and counted out eleven dollars. That was to pay for Dan! We muttered to ourselves that it was an awful lot of money, and we already had babies. What a waste spending all that money. Eleven dollars! Sometimes I look at Dan now, and think, *eleven dollars!*"

Edna: "Our little brother Dan was a slow walker. He was content to get around as babies will, but put off life's first big responsibility, that of learning to walk! I was eight years old. Already, I was a helper for Mama in watching the little ones, and I took Dan as a project, to teach him how to walk. So we walked....and walked...and walked."

BABY BROTHER'S WALKING LESSONS
(Dan)

Sister was Mama's chief helper
With a baby always on the place.
She tended them in and out of the house,
Where she was needed in any case.

Baby Brother, then, was almost ready
For the wonderful stage of walking.
Sister set out to speed it along
And started a determined program.
(Continued)

45

She'd stand him up in front of her
With a grip on each little arm,
Walk him along in tiny steps
Hoping that soon he'd catch on.

She did that diligently every day
In the yard and all around.
His baby legs would get so tired,
He'd just sit down in the sand.

Sister worked the plan for weeks!
Baby Brother was getting the notion,
That the way out of this daily routine
Was to put his legs to walking...

During those days on a Sunday,
Uncle and Aunt came visiting
And while cousin was playing with Baby,
He just toddled off...walking!

Sister watched with speechless delight,
Thankful for what effort had wrought
When Uncle, without inquiry, announced:
"Look! Cousin taught Baby to walk!"

Anyway, Brother grew up to be
The tallest of the lot.
Could be that he was stretched out a bit
From the early walking lessons he got.

Note: Our brother Dan, among his other talents, is an author now with several successful novels to his credit. He wrote a little article for me, at my request, to summarize the momentous time in his life as he went through this ordeal of learning how to walk at his big sister's insistence.

Dan: "On the matter of Edna teaching me to walk, I considered the prospect and rejected the new configuration of upright locomotion for the following reasons:
1.) When standing, one is quite a ways from the floor. If something goes wrong, it will come up and smack you!
2.) If you do the sensible thing and use the hands and knees system, you can easily reach down and touch the floor anytime you wish or even kiss it if you need assurance.
3.) However, after much encouragement and many kamikaze dives to the floor, I finally recognized the mobile advantage and the much better view of up-right locomotion."

Note: Musical talent is scattered through the ten Holt children. Daddy and Mama had talent that was never tapped or developed in any way. I used to think *"What a waste that my parents never had the advantage of education and developing of their talents."* But as I grew in the knowledge of God, I realized that He often takes the disadvantages and turns them to develop the lives that will fulfill His divine purpose. Our parents enjoyed their musical gifts in their children, and grandchildren.

John, the sixth child, and fourth son of Daddy and Mama did, by hard work and perseverance, develop his musical talent. He earned a degree in sacred music and served as a Music Director in several churches. In addition, he taught music in a Baptist College for a time. Various interest and talents sometimes begin to show up early in a child's life.

RECOLLECTION

(John)

The family considered it beautiful,
The simple chords that Sister made
On the old upright piano...
And they were certainly entertained.

Little Brother, always fascinated,
Would press his ear to the imposing end
And listen in childish wonder,
With a longing words can't explain.

The music vibrated his slight frame
And spilled into his being,
Discovering a source of potential
Suitable for its revealing.

Decades of living and learning are past.
He has led choirs magnificent!
And taught music and heavenly harmony,
Ever drawing from that potential.

Could it be that source will ever deplete?
Never! It's a bubbling spring
That began one day when little Brother
Pressed an ear for the music...and listened.

Note: When Daddy was terminally ill in1979, John arranged a special gift of music for him, though John was in another state.

John: "In East Texas, I remember many times Daddy would get up early and make coffee and sit at the table and drink coffee and listen to the Stamps Quartet, on Station KRLD out of Dallas, sing gospel quartet music for 15 minutes from 5:15 to 5:30 in the morning. They would sing and read verses of scripture they called Precious Promises. Daddy would sing with them. Their theme song was *Give The World A Smile*.

"In 1979 when we lived in Massillon, Ohio, I taught music in the college and had a group of singers on tour when Daddy was in the hospital for the last time. I was in Florida and I called Daddy in the hospital and had my young men's quartet sing *Give The World A Smile* from a phone booth for Daddy. His voice was weak but he said it was sure a beautiful song for him to hear."

Note: My brother, Frank, spoke at our Mother's funeral. At the time he told about the incident later described in the family poem, *The Littlest Cowboy*. That was the first I'd heard it, so I hurriedly scribbled the facts as I understood them. Later I wrote the poem with Frank as the little cowboy in it! Actually, there were *two* little cowboys involved. I'll leave the poem intact, but let Mack relate the *real* story and we can easily imagine the facts.

Mack: "Frank and I *ran together* on the farm, which means we got in most of the trouble together! Like the time Daddy made us some stick horses. We rode those horses until our tongues were hanging out!

"One day we tied the horses to the front porch and went in the house for a drink. Mama was sewing some clothes so the machine was set up in the living room. On our way back out we noticed a large new spool of white thread on the spindle on top of the machine. For some reason Frank took it and slid it over the nail on his horse's head, tied the end to the porch post and we took off around the house. That thread was unrolling 90 miles an hour! About the second or third time around the house the thread ran out and left the spool spinning on that nail.

"We both stopped and suddenly realized that we had made an extremely poor decision! We dropped the horses and tried to re-wind the thread on the spool. Frank was rolling and I was going ahead pulling the thread out of the weeds, spider webs and dirt. It wasn't long before the thread was about 3 inches in diameter with dirt, twigs and leaves!

"As we came to the front porch Mama was waiting with a peach tree switch in hand. She jerked Frank up on her lap and started giving him a full dose! I knew I was next so I just started crying as Frank was yelling: *'Mama we'll fix it, we'll fix it!'* Mama said something like, *'You can't fix it; we'll have to get a new one.'* That was one of many lessons I learned on the farm: Be careful what you break; some things can't be fixed!"

THE LITTLEST COWBOY
(Frank and Mack)

He was thirsty and his horse all lathered,
So he tied him to the porch hitching post,
Having ridden out all the country,
As far as he was allowed to go.

Not an Indian was left in hiding,
Or an outlaw or wildcat or wolf
That he hadn't got rid of bravely
Astraddle his thoroughbred stick horse.

As he went through the house to the kitchen,
He spied Mama's sewing machine
With the biggest spool of white thread
His childish eyes had ever seen.

There was the finest rope in the country!
He hung it on the nail nose of his horse.
It galloped off with fresh new vigor
With the thread end tied to the porch.

He made two trips around the house
Before that good rope came to its end.
Thinking how many varmints he could tie up,
His ears heard, "FRANKIE ...COME IN!

He thought of heading for the border,
But at supper he'd have to be here,
So he galloped up to face Mama
Yelling, "I'LL FIX IT BACK ON THERE!"

He hurriedly wound it up tightly
With leaves, twigs, dirt, and trash.
It turned out big as a baseball!
Pitiful sight...he could tell by Mama's face.

(Continued)

Well, he took his spanking bravely
Listening for Mama's advice:
"You can't always fix what you tangle,
So be careful what you do in life."

That stick horse lasted him a long time,
With that nail for turning its head.
Brother never hung another thing on it...
Just used it for guiding instead.

Note: Mama never wrote a book, nor did she ever read one on how to raise a houseful of little boys. But she had the basic principles down right. With love she also wielded the peach tree switch (her apparent favorite) as discipline was needed. Her efforts produced outstanding results. Though she did not know it at the time, she and Daddy were raising successful, resourceful citizens.

Among them would be writers, preachers, a school teacher, a pastor's wife, a music director, business men, a career Army officer and a missionary: our brother Frank, who served for many years in Papua, New Guinea.

He and Beverly endured hardships getting through Bible College where they prepared to serve as foreign Missionaries. Already a licensed pilot in his teens, he went on to become an instructor, which helped him through the lean (sometimes hilarious) times of college years.

Frank: "While in Baptist Bible College I taught flying at the local airport to pay the bills. When the weather was too bad to fly, I would sell pots and pans out of town on Friday night and Saturday. On one of those late Saturday night drives back to the College apartment, my Volkswagen Beetle quit on a lonely country road.

"It was near midnight and I thought I was stuck till the next day, but another student came by in a big Oldsmobile and seeing me, stopped to help. We decided to tow the VW behind the Olds. We looked for something to hookup; wire from a nearby fence; nothing; no rope; chain.

"We finally found an old Army blanket in the trunk of the Olds. We kept moving the VW closer to his bumper to tie a knot in the Army blanket. We soon learned that Army blanket knots are about the size of a 3 gallon bucket, so the knots in the blanket took up all the blanket and the cars ended up bumper to bumper.

"I told my friend to drive slow and we could make our way (another 40 miles) to town. Soon, this theological A. J. Foyt (the famous race car driver) was cruising 70 mph on that two lane blacktop with me riding the brakes and staring at his license plate a scant 6 feet away, passing cars in our duo arrangement.

"Pulling into the college about 1:00 AM, the blanket was now 6 feet long between the bumpers and the knots are softball size. After a night's sleep, we took screwdrivers and pried the knots apart and tossed the blanket on the ground which took a diamond shape and was no longer rectangular. Beetle Bailey could not have slept on it!"

Note: The youngest five of my brothers were small children when I got married. I have fond memories of doing the little things that a big sister does in the family. Seeing that their clothes were ready for school and church, and the simple daily routines of washing their faces and combing their hair before mealtime was all *big sister's* responsibility.

LITTLE BROTHER'S APPEAL
(Mack)

The beautiful dresser set came one day,
Shining with gold-rimmed edging.
It contained a brush, mirror, and comb;
A gift he'd chosen with consideration.

It was placed on my bedroom dresser,
Adding a special touch to the room.
It was admired with fancy by all the boys
Especially little brother, four years in bloom.

He'd wash his face and hands just so
Then appear at my bedroom door,
And with the greatest appeal he could muster:
"Ahna, I want your mo t'comb my ha."

(Edna, I want your mirror to comb my hair)

He considered each use special,
Carefully handling the mirror and comb.
It sure beat what others used...
This was Sister's, and glittering gold!

Little Brother grew up to have some class;
We don't know where all he got it.
The first step may have been right there...
"Ahna, I want your mo t'comb my ha."

Note: Mack did grow up to *have some class* and achieved his life's dream to become a pilot. He has a long list of impressive accomplishments to his credit. It could be that it all started back on that little East Texas farm many years ago.

Mack: "When I was about 7 or 8 I remember the Air Force B-52 Bombers that used to fly over the farm on their practice runs. Frank and I used to talk about flying and wondered what it was like way up in the sky like that.

One day Jack, Dan, John, Frank and a neighbor and I had an afternoon off from the fields. So, the older brothers decided to build an airplane. They took some old pieces of barn wood and nailed them together in the right shape. They put on a cockpit (an apple crate I think) and cut some tin in the shape of a propeller and nailed it to the front so it would turn when the wind hit it.

"Since I was the smallest, they put me in the cockpit, lifted the airplane up high and started running toward the back of the house. The wind was blowing my little blond hair and I was gripping that stick in the cockpit! The propeller was turning and clanking and to me it seemed like I was really flying!

"I often tell people that in my little 8 year old mind THAT FLIGHT was as real to me as the one that got me my Commercial Pilot's License 15 years later!"

Note: In my pre-teen years, the family had moved to a farm in West Texas. It was in this place where I finally got my baby sister! I was 12 years old and though I knew more about life, I felt that Dicey *not* being there probably helped.

THE PINK SATIN ROCKER
(Connie)

When Little Sister was born that night,
The household was very pleased.
Daddy and Mama were also delighted,
That the new baby was a 'she'.

It had been so long since we had one,
I had no recollection...
For between me and baby Sister
Were five strapping boys growing!

Mama had her heart's desire set
For a thing she felt was fitting.
So with boys galore, and a baby girl,
She got a pink satin rocker for sitting.

Sister was Mama's little princess;
A satin rocking chair was the need.
We considered it the greatest thing too
Taking turns on that satin seat.

The room was kept clean around it,
Dusted, and the window wiped clear,
For the sun to stream in on its beauty.
We were motivated all that year.

We rocked with our wandering fancies
Wherever our thoughts were led.
That chair could have graced a mansion,
But brightened our corner instead.

Note: This book is dedicated to the memory of Bruce, and our parents. He had the distinction of being the only Holt sibling born in a hospital, in November of 1950.

THE LITTLEST BROTHER
(Bruce)

Providence dealt me a trying blow
When my slot was selected
To be the last one of the lot
Of offspring our parents collected.

The house was full when I arrived;
All had their own places and things.
I was surrounded like a stranger,
Who had stumbled in out of the rain.

"Where did you come from? What is your name?
And what are you doing there?"
I snuggled closer to Mama,
Rocking me in her chair.

Daddy was as proud as the first time
To have another son.
He bought Mama a bouquet of flowers,
The day they brought me home.

Sister had the house spruced up,
Making everything extra clean.
She guessed I'd be the last one,
Rounding it off at ten.

I don't mind now being a part
Of a family strung out like a train.
I'd like being closer to the engine though,
Than to be the caboose of the thing.

CHRISTMAS ON THE JUDD PLACE

We knew it was coming by the aroma
From the kitchen about two weeks before.
Mama started baking pies and cakes...
All of them to be stored!

She filled the shelves of the pantry
In the back room of the house.
The sweet odor bettered day by day:
The delightful smell of Christmas!

Our uncles, aunts, and cousins
Arrived in a holiday flurry.
At night the kids built a bonfire,
And huddled around it telling stories.

Sister loved to tell ghostly tales,
Making everybody's hair stand up!
Then there were yarns about Santa,
And his toys, candy, and nuts.

We'd keep the fire going till late
On Christmas Eve and watch the sky,
Pretending we expected to see Old Nick;
The little ones were all 'ears and eyes'.

By then we had tasted of Mama's horde
Of cakes and pies and the like...
Beside, there were oranges and apples,
And other stuff for tasting delights.

It's amazing how we ever made room
For so many others eating and sleeping.
None remembered the inconveniences though,
While making Christmas memories for keeping.

Note: During this period of time is when my life changed forever. I had been writing to my *pen-pal* for over two years, and when he came home from the Korean War for an extended furlough, he came straight to Texas, from Illinois, and within a week of first seeing each other, we got married! My husband tells our unusual story in the Family Memories book.

Louis: "It seems like I slipped into the family through the mailbox, since Edna and I had been writing to each other for two years, without ever meeting each other. In February, 1948, her cousin, Charles Holt, and I were sworn into the U.S. Army together at Love Field in Dallas, Texas.

"After basic training in California, we were shipped out to Japan prior to the war in Korea. I had no one writing to me except my Mom, so Charles suggested that I write to his cousin, Edna Holt, in Oklaunion, Texas. I did, and that started a letter writing campaign that led to matrimony.

"When I came home from Korea in late May of 1951, I called her on the phone and heard her voice for the first time. We agreed that I would come to Texas to see her. I traveled by Greyhound Bus from Benton, Illinois to Oklaunion where she met me at the Bus Station. It was on Tuesday about 2:00 AM in the morning when I saw, for the first time, this girl who would be my wife."

Note: Louis and I exchanged hundreds of letters, and I'd read many to the family. They knew him as well as I did, and the boys admired him because he was a COMBAT soldier. He had experience in the war. I had no idea how they would react when he actually came in person.

I know that my baby sister, Connie, who was 4 years old at the time, was very upset when Louis told her he was taking me home with him. That was not good news to Connie and my little brothers; that I would be leaving home to go with this soldier. They would miss *big sister*. I was, in many ways, like a *nanny* doing many things for them.

THE SOLDIER
(Dan, John, Frank, Mack)

Sister wrote letters for several years
To her Soldier...quite a hero,
Waiting and wondering until the day
The call came: *"I'll be there tomorrow!"*

Keen was the excitement of the family,
But we are disappointed yet.
He arrived ready for courting,
Not with a rifle and fixed bayonet!

First, we heard his pockets jingle;
That was good news to our ears.
The way he looked at Sister,
We could have fleeced him for years.

Empty jars around the house
Were quickly prepared for collecting:
Cutting narrow slots in the lids...
Respectable, just right for soliciting.

We lined up morning and evening,
And looked him straight in the eye,
Shook our jars nodding toward Sister,
And he contributed without a sigh.

That Soldier took our sister away;
We didn't understand it at the time.
But we certainly made him appreciate her:
He left there without a dime!

THE CHAPERONE
(Jack)

It fell Brother's lot and duty
A few days from Sister getting married
To accompany the two of them out at night,
Chaperoning her and her 'intended'.

Daddy was strictly old-fashioned;
He knew that from past learning,
But couldn't figure for the life of him
Why anyone could be concerned.

Sister could well take care of herself;
He had seen her on several occasions,
Line up and whop every kid on the place
And scream like a panther if she had reason.

If a guy had come along
Who didn't know Sister was a lady,
She'd have whacked him up beside the head,
And explained it to him...not so kindly.

Well, he was here guarding her honor,
Now worried, he enjoyed the eats;
Then stayed alert as he could be
In the back seat, fast asleep.

Edna: "Bruce was the last one of the *younger ones* and so I did not have a lot of interaction with him growing up. However, there was naturally a bond there and as he matured in adulthood I admired his ability to do well in life. He developed his own construction company and at one time when he was working on a huge mansion in Dallas, he invited his three sisters to come see it, in the process, and afterwards he would take us to lunch.

"Neecie, Connie and I met him at this building site where he gave us the tour. Never had I seen such a beautiful place where people actually would live! I wondered how in the world Bruce *knew* how to build such a place. After viewing that wonder, he took us to a nice place where we enjoyed lunch together.

"A few weeks before Bruce died; he was in the hospital coping with the last stages of cancer that had devastated his body. Louis and I went to see him one day. When we walked in Bruce started working his way through the many wires and hookup things to sit up on the side of the bed. His wife, Elaine, asked *'What are you doing?'* He replied with a strong voice as he stood up by the bed; *'I'm going to stand up and hug my sister!'* And he did!

"I'll always remember that last hug I got from my baby brother."

Note: After Bruce was born and I had gotten married, the family settled back on their East Texas farm and the children began to grow up with many varied experiences.

Mack: "I will never forget that mean old rooster we had; I think his names was Tom, that would chase us if we got too close to his chickens. One day Frank and I and Connie were trying to get to the house for dinner but the rooster kept chasing us. Connie cried so Frank came up with a PLAN. He decided that he and I would run around the house so Tom would chase us, and then Connie would run in the house and tell Mama so she would come out and rescue us from the rooster. We ran, Tom chased, Connie ran to the house....but, she forgot to tell Mama! After several times around that little farm house, we were losing ground to Tom so we started yelling for Mama.

"The next time we rounded the back corner of the house Mama was waiting with her broom over her shoulder, like Babe Ruth, the baseball player. When Tom came around, Mama hit a home run! Feathers flew! Tom landed about 20 feet out in the yard. First time I ever saw a rooster fly backwards!"

THE ROOSTER

(Frank, Mack, Connie)

He strutted his best behavior
When Mama was in the yard.
The minute she was out of sight
Little Sister and the boys put on their guard.

That hateful bird would chase them,
Intending to peck if he could.
He seemed to know their childish fright,
And lorded it over them good.

They fervently wished toward Sunday
That Mama would choose him then
And ring his head right off his neck
And cook Rooster instead of a hen.

One day the children managed
To slip past him out to play.
When returning, the rooster was waiting
To give them a fright for the day.

(Continued)

The boys offered to be decoys;
Little Sister could slip by the brute.
They took off running around the house
With the rooster in hot pursuit!

They'd instructed Sister to tell Mama,
When she was safe inside
To come out and rescue them
From getting peck marks on their hides!

Little Sister escaped as planned,
But forgot to tell Mama the facts.
The boys were running their breath out
With Rooster close in their tracks!

Their calls for help fading in and out
As they circled past front and back
Refreshed Little Sister's memory...
Mama quickly interrupted Rooster's attack.

She whacked him with the broom
And ran him back to the chicken pen.
The boys wished Mama had wrung his neck
And cooked Rooster for Sunday, instead of a hen.

Note: Within a year after Louis and I married, we came to visit the family on this farm. Farming was totally unknown to my husband, so it was amusing to the family as he tried to learn some things while he was there. This farm was still in the old-fashioned mode of operation. It was a challenge for a *city boy*.

LEARNING TO PLOW
(Jack and Louis)

It was spring plowing time
When Sister and husband came back.
It was their first visit home;
They were welcomed with delight.

Brother hooked the mules up early
And plowed in the field each day.
Brother-in-law, with his inquiring mind,
Desired to know how it worked that way.

The plow was guided so easily
Around stumps up and down rows.
The team, ole Biggun and Kate,
Pulled it patiently and rather slow.

Following Brother around the rows
The stranger to plowing asked a turn.
Brother handed the plow-lines to him,
And stepped aside to watch him learn.

In-Law took off behind the plow,
The mules stepping lightly...a sight!
Quick time was made on a single row;
Tired out, he handed it back.
"I don't understand how you plow,
With so little effort and sweat;
With doing one round I'm exhausted;
You've got the whole day yet."

Brother grinned with understanding;
The episode had made his day.
"I let the mules pull the plow;
You pushed it yourself...all the way."

LITTLE SISTER'S SOLUTION

(Connie and Mack)

Little Sister knew she was favored
Being among so many brothers.
But she certainly didn't appreciate
Not getting the same as the others.

For Daddy brought the boys chewing gum,
And a candy sucker is what she got.
She didn't want that delicacy;
It was chewing gum she liked a lot!

She thought of a devious plan one day,
Knowing the brother she could outrun.
As soon as Daddy passed out the treats,
She tried first to trade for the gum.

That didn't work, so she tackled like a pro
With little brother hollering in vain!
She took his gum from between his teeth,
And left her sucker in exchange.

That became Little Sister's solution;
She was not going to be outdone.
Each time Daddy brought her a sucker,
She made Brother exchange his gum.

He'd frantically try to chew it good,
But Sister was never dismayed.
She'd sit on his chest and take the gum
And leave the sucker in his mouth instead!

Note: Connie was brought up among her brothers, the only girl. One of her most memorable experiences was when Daddy accidentally backed over her with the pick-up when she was three. She always wanted to go when the chores were being done. She relates a time when Daddy and the boys were going to feed the pigs, away from the house.

Connie: "Well on this particular day, I had made enough of a fuss that Daddy let me go. Of course, riding in the cab of the pickup wouldn't do. I had to be in the back with the boys. Daddy reluctantly said '*okay,*' if I would sit between the boys. He warned them that they must hold on tight to me so I wouldn't fall out.

"The adventure went just fine. We made it to the pigpen. I watched from the back of the truck as Daddy and the boys fed the pigs, and I eagerly sat between them as we prepared for the drive back to the house. Naturally, I had to sit on the tailgate and swing my legs just like the big brothers were doing. Just as Daddy put the truck into reverse, the clutch jerked. I tumbled out over the tailgate just as Daddy got the truck into reverse, and he began to back up over me.

"Fortunately, I was not under a tire, or I wouldn't be here typing today! I was hit by the end of the tailpipe that caused me to be curled up into a little ball under the truck! Almost simultaneously the boys begin to scream for Daddy to stop and pull up, which he quickly did. I remember being picked up in his strong arms and carefully being taken to the cab of the pickup. I remember how very scared and white Daddy's face was, as he looked me over carefully to make sure I was alright. With the exception of a small red burn on my lower back, I was miraculously fine. God was so good to me that day! My final memory of that day was Daddy driving very slowly back to the house with trembling hands on the wheel of the pickup. I don't know if any of the boys got a *whooping* after that, but I do remember not getting to go anywhere for quite awhile."

TRIBUTE TO MY SISTERS

My two sisters are truly my life-long friends. Though we are years apart, it turned out to be a great advantage to us in time, for we had Neecie's maturity with us while ours was still in the *bud* and in our older waning years we have had Connie's youth and vitality. She has made our *sister trips* a delight as she could arrange things and drive us all over the country for our special times together. Neecie was seven years old when I was born, and the only living person now who remembers that day. I was near thirteen years old when Connie was born and I've written the poem THE NIGHT YOU WERE BORN about that special event and the night which I'll never forget.

Connie has been a school-teacher all of her adult life. She loves that work and is very dedicated to it as well as being dedicated to the Lord in her church and its ministry. Most recently, Connie had her first book, an entertaining novel for youth, published. Her students have delighted in reading it at school.

Neecie is unique in her role as the matriarch of our family since both our parents are deceased. Even after having a stroke in 2006, she has kept up with communication and had a positive influence.

I wrote the poem, A THOUGHT FOR NEECIE, after her debilitating stroke which impaired her left side. She has faithfully attended church in spite of her handicap, and has thrived in faith. During my young years as a pastor's wife, she was my encourager through those early *learning* times. She assisted with finding bargains and sewing for the children when our income, at first, was very meager. And when the inevitable *ripples of trouble* came occasionally, Neecie's sage advice was always *"Sit steady in the boat."* Her confidence helped mine to develop as I learned and grew in the things of the Lord...and in the role of a pastor's wife.

A THOUGHT FOR NEECIE

Without experience we have a limited view of life,
With numerous distortions barely brushing reality
Until our own world turns upside down and we are
Trapped under the wreckage
Of all that was normal and routine.

Hope survived the wreckage!
And bids you make new goals.
It sings while you work. Listen!

Despair viewed the wreckage with morbid intent,
Pawing through debris, pointing out devastation,
Hinting for a place in your life.

Bitterness tags along with a subtle kind of comfort
As it endeavors to get a strangle-hold
On the tender part of your heart,
And turn it to stone.

Keep your eyes on hope!
It's the one standing pointing upward
To the hills 'from which cometh your help'.
Capture the scene in your mind
Where imagination and understanding are intact.

You can and you will!
You can do 'all things' through Christ,
From whose presence
Despair and bitterness slither away.

THE NIGHT YOU WERE BORN

(Connie)

I was there the night you were born
Keeping the rest of the 'flock'
In the adjoining room.

On that cold winter night, time suspended;
I could sense it, and wondered
At the mystery still closed to me.

Little ones were soothed back to slumber
As they stirred in the night
Cradled in my arms.

I scarcely breathed, knowing a miracle
Was unfolding so close, yet
So far away of my understanding

Quieting...soothing...waiting...
Weariness closed my eyes.

Daylight was edging through the window
As I was awakened with startling news:
A baby sister!

And so it was.
You changed our lives.
I remember the night you were born.

TO CONNIE

As God chose me, He chose you too
To encourage and bless
As I journey through.

Though a decade's between us,
God's design brought us near
And we are joined on the journey
Of my life's waning years.

At times seeing darkly
In the glare of God's light,
You helped me to focus...
To see clearly in 'faith' sight.

As God chose me, He chose you too
To encourage and bless
As I journey through.

TO NEECIE

Our friendship deepens
As years go by,
And the richer are we...
Especially me
Since you've always been there
To steady me up
And help me to see.

CHRISTMAS TREE QUILT
(A gift for Connie)

We would love to give you some rare gift
Like sparkling jewels, velvets, or delicate silks.
Instead, with older awkwardly hands,
We planned and made a Christmas tree quilt.

Its warmth and color will always declare
How we appreciate, love you and really care
That Christmas is your season of personal delight,
And Christmas trees a favorite thing in your sight.

The reds are bright and the greens are green,
Yet it's not only for the Christmas scene.
It will brighten any day, as ours shall be,
Knowing you'll enjoy a quilt of Christmas trees.

Note: Since her stroke, Neecie and I have exchanged letters, handwritten letters, almost daily through the years. When they pile up we return our letters to each other and have them spiral bound, making a book of letters preserved and convenient to review. We each have volumes of a diary of our lives spanning several years: a treasure for our children and grandchildren. But meanwhile, it is our delight to have personal, handwritten, letters to enjoy often. An excerpt from a May 2007 letter reads:

"Dear Neecie,   I finally got a letter from you today and glad to get it. The bumblebees are still guarding the mailbox, hovering around the porch like little fat helicopters! Folks go in and out in a hurry and the mailman dashes in, picks up your letter out of the box, and takes off again....."

LETTERS

I like to write at crack of dawn
With fresh coffee aroma sparking the day.
And my desire to share my thoughts,
Whether shallow or deep, it matters not;
Personally written, they are treasures to keep.

It seems to be single conversation,
But only so, for in stacks of letters
Hoarded in time, she speaks to me
Line after line.

Could ever such a prize be found
As a bundle of old letters
In a grandmother's realm...
Extraordinary, handwritten history intact;
How quaint the expressions of folks way back.

More than unique, our thoughts
Inscribed week after week reveals a life:
It's broad and narrow...a relief to know,
And in some measure show
Who we are.

I like to write at crack of dawn!
Or any time handy to paper and pen.
Whatever the thoughts sent daily along
They are welcomed and treasured
Again...and again.

EDNA HOLMES

MEMORIES

TO

KEEP

Memories From

the Holt Kids

Note: The first four of the Holt children, *the older ones*, have quite different memories to relate of their childhood than *the younger ones*. The stories that Neecie and Willie can tell are as interesting, even fascinating, history of those times. They can relate more about Mama's and Daddy's younger years as they started out, not really knowing where they wanted to settle down permanently. The first two siblings were born in West Texas out near Lubbock on a big farm ranch where Daddy worked for a few years. He and Mama got homesick for familiar territory and a place where there were no sandstorms. Then, they moved back to East Texas.

A few years ago our family compiled a book of memories with each one of us contributing our recollections of things in our childhood days. It is far from complete but from those writings, I've gleaned more bits and pieces of our family history, and am sharing them as MEMORIES TO KEEP. Even the *younger ones* of the ten of us are amazed at the difference that two decades made in the changes that came about in our times. Our oldest sister, Neecie, wrote the most comprehensive narrative about the early days of the family. I'll use her writings extensively in this section for the clearest descriptions of living in that time period.

Both of our parents lost their mothers when they were children. My Dad was 12 years old, and Mama was 9 years old. Both had very difficult times growing up without their mothers to nourish them, and prepare them for life as mothers do. Daddy had been making his way in the world for several years, because he was a good worker, and didn't have a lazy part in him. Mama had hardly been off the farm when she married Daddy. The first years would prove to be interesting to say the least. They were so different in temperament and personality. Mama shared so much about their early life with Neecie, and we all are so glad she did now. Otherwise, we would never know these things.

Sometime in the first year of marriage the house they had rented burned down. Daddy had managed to get a car, a 1917 Ford and so they traveled about, mostly in West Texas where they had relatives.

Neecie: "Daddy had gone to West Texas when he first left home as a young man, 18 or 19 years old. He worked in a feed mill in Amarillo and later farm work, pulling bolls which he was very good at; pulling 1000 to 1200 pounds a day. Mama said that one day in competing with another fellow he pulled 2000 pounds. But that was a long hard day and he never did that again.

"Daddy wouldn't let Mama work in the fields. She was very small and frail, weighing less than 100 lbs. She said that Daddy would take her to town on Saturday to the beauty shop and she would get a *Marcel*, a forerunner of the perms, which lasted for weeks.

"Then Dad would buy lunch for them and take her to see a movie, a western of course. Mama said that most of the time he would not go in, or if he did, he wouldn't stay. He just didn't care for it. My guess is Daddy didn't care for entertainment unless he was the one entertaining! Mama said he would chat with the old men who hung around the square or tinker with his car while she was in the movie. It was a nice looking car; a four door. Mama dressed nicely in the 1920's style and she had a picture of her and Daddy beside the car.

"Mama had never seen movies before so she must have felt like a kid on Saturday. Years later when Willie and I were kids, 8 and 9 years old, Mama would tell us about the Westerns she saw. She could recall the plots and stars exactly. We heard about Tom Mix, Buck Jones, Bob Steele, Hoot Gibson, and Tim McCoy and others before we ever saw a movie. She was a good narrator and it was a magical time for us on rainy days or long winter evenings beside the fire."

Note: On their 50th wedding anniversary, Mama wrote about their early years of marriage. She recalls them traveling in that old 1917 Ford *"all over the western part of Texas,"* and then they had reason to settle down. I quote this segment of her writings:

Mama: "We did not have any arguments until I got pregnant the first time. We stopped in Lubbock while moving from Plainview to Tahoka. I wanted a hat, but was ashamed to get out because I was pregnant. He hopped out and went in the store and bought me an old blue hat. It looked like a chamber-pot. I took it off my head and threw in out into the street. He ran and got it and took it back in the store and got his money back. I went on without a hat."

Neecie: "When I was a baby, Mama and Daddy took me to a show with them. It was a live show (Harley-Sadler tent shows) with skits and comedy and a regular full length play. In between scenes, they would have a singer to entertain while the cast changed costumes. The singer was a young unknown named Gene Autry! I was six months old and was restless and whining so they took turns holding me, trying to keep me quiet so they could enjoy the show. Mama took off her wedding ring and gave it to me to play with and I dropped it in the sawdust. After the show, they crawled around looking for it and other people helped look, but they never found it."

Note: Years later, Neecie would have a ring made for Mama which *replaced* the lost wedding ring. Mama wore it the rest of her life. Neecie's granddaughter now has the prized ring.

Neecie: "Mama told me that in this place, when I was about 2 years old, when the horses would gather around the water trough to drink, I'd slip under the fence and push the horses apart, go through and stand with them and dabble my hands in the water. If I couldn't push them apart to get to the trough, I'd walk under their stomachs.

"They never paid me any mind, never stepped on me, and Mama would just have a fit when she saw it, and wanted Daddy to go in there and get me. He was afraid the horses would spook and hurt me accidentally if he came over the fence. So, I'm guessing that he told me to be still and let the horses drink, then they would drift away from the trough. All I remember is dabbling my hands in the water and horses all around me."

Neecie "In the wintertime, I'd follow Mama out to the garden, and I've watched her break ice off the collard greens and cut them off at the base. Mama told me she always had trouble with me slipping out behind her and following anywhere she'd go; so when it was too cold for me to be out she would set the bedpost on my dress so I'd stay put while she ran outside for whatever reason. Mama also did that when I started crawling because I'd try to pull up to the stove. She'd set the bedpost on the tail of my dress.

"We had a 1917 Ford touring car. It had a canvas top and *Ising Glass*, a kind of substitute for glass. If it was rainy or cold, you could pull them down and they hooked. Then they could be rolled up and tied with a cord. When we moved back to east Texas we came in the car.

"Willie and I sat in the back seat on a stack of quilts. We came through Ft. Worth, as we went over an overpass; I thought people were driving under the ground. The cars were so simple then. If it broke down, Daddy would get a piece of wire off the fence and fix it. The battery set on the running board. No heater. It took us three days to make that trip. We stayed 3 nights in tourist courts."

Note: As Neecie continues her narrative, I'm struck with the gradual change of so many things. I barely remember the motels being called *Tourist Courts*. And in the era of the 1920's there were none of the modern conveniences to keep babies entertained, safe, and healthy etc. The mother would indeed put the baby's dress tail under a bedpost (usually in the living room) to keep it safe while she did her necessary chores.

Neecie: "I don't know exactly why Daddy and Mama left Tahoka for East Texas. It must have been in early 1931. Willie would have been about two years old. Maybe the sandstorms and drought was part of it. What history calls *The Dust Bowl Era* started in 1929 and lasted 10 years. It devastated parts of 5 states. Lubbock and Tahoka were included in that area. I remember the sandstorms. One of my earliest memories is standing with my face pressed to the screen door watching an approaching sandstorm. Someone pulled me back and closed the door and put a towel at the bottom.

"I can also remember Mama sweeping big piles of sand across the floor and out the door and wiping sand off of the furniture and window sills and washing bed clothes. There was sand in everything. I guess to two people raised in East Texas with trees, forest, creeks, rivers and lush grass, it must have seemed like a desert. Mama would have hated sand in everything...everywhere.

"So back they came to Blakney and the little house on the bank of Red River. It had once been a nice place I think; it had a concrete walk in front out to the road. Mama planted zinnias on both sides of the walk and they grew higher than my head. Mama called them *old maids*, and called iris *flags*. The old folks had their own names for flowers. They passed seeds around to each other for generations without ever knowing the proper name for them. They planted hollyhocks around hen houses for shade and sunflowers along fences for chicken feed.

"The river flooded while we lived there. On our side the bluffs were caving in at intervals along the shore. Our house being only about a hundred and fifty yards from the river, Daddy built a huge bonfire at night on the edge of the bluffs in view of their bedroom window. He knew if the bluff caved in there, the firelight disappearing would awaken him.

The view of the river down from the bluff looked like water boiling in the surge of the flooding waters. On the Texas side, it was the high bank and bluffs, and on the

Oklahoma side, it was more sloping, beach like, so more flooding occurred on that side.

"From there we moved to Oklahoma. We moved in a wagon that had bows over it, and Daddy stretched a canvas over and we thought we were in a covered wagon. We had to drive down to Albion and cross on the ferry. Daddy had rented a farm near Rufe, Oklahoma. But though he made some good crops, the depression was on and there was no market for anything.

"One of my first memories of that place was seeing Daddy come riding out of the woods with a deer across the saddle. People couldn't get food to eat. Daddy even killed a wild hog in the woods.

"Mama miscarried (twin boys) at six months. Malaria was rampant, and Mama was sick a lot. She picked up a feather bed to take out for airing on the porch, and after that she went into premature labor, and after some time the twins were stillborn. We are told that Daddy took them out and buried them. There was a little cemetery nearby.

"Little River was not far from us and one day on an outing, Daddy swam across it with me on his back! Then he took Willie and swam across and back. Little River was clear as crystal and you could see the bottom.

"Edna was born there in Rufe, Oklahoma. Daddy came in one day from the field and told us to come with him over to the Spencer's place and play with their kids. We were out playing at the creek and Mrs. Spencer, who helped Mama deliver the baby, came out and got her kids and told us we had a baby sister. We ran to the house and Daddy took us in and showed us the baby. *'You've got a baby sister,'* He said. We probably asked Daddy where she came from and he might have said they found me on the creek bank. Anyway, later on Willie and I told Edna that little story.

"Mama and Daddy were having hard times. Their stock (animals) died because there was no food. It was drought all over Oklahoma and Texas. That was the period of the Dust Bowl days when times were desperately hard for everybody. A lot of people left and went to California, or other places.

"Seems like things gradually got a little better, but we were always having relatives come to our house when nobody else would take them in. Mama's mean eccentric Uncle Johnny came with his old goat and a little wiry dog. He was not welcome anywhere because everyone hated him but Mama and Daddy, who felt a little compassion because of his absolutely homeless situation. He had never been married and was mean and hateful to everybody.

"Uncle Johnny's old goat was as mean as he was, and he terrorized me and Willie if we got near him. He was penned in the back pasture that we had to go through to get to the Spencers, and that goat would run at us every time we got over the fence.

"When we complained to Mama one day, she said *'Just put a tub over your heads and the goat won't bother you.'* Sure enough, when we put a tub over us, both holding it up and walking along, the goat ran to the far corner of the pen and stayed there. We were delighted and than for a pastime fun, we'd get under the tub and walk around scaring the goat."

Note: When I was a baby, Daddy and Mama moved back across the Red River to Blakney, and a few years later to the Little's Place. Willie relates how industrious Daddy was with what he had to work with.

Willie: "When I was about ten, we moved to Greenwood, to the Little's Place, and farmed there for about four years. Dad was a hustler, and soon had a blacksmith shop, a grist-mill, and a syrup-mill. I remember one time when we were making syrup, Dad would skim the top of the juice, and put it in a little ditch we had dug to carry it to a little pool about 35 feet away. The skimmings would ferment and the hogs would drink it. One day the hogs got so drunk, they could not stand up.

"When we ran the cane through the mill we would throw it in a stack (they were called pummies) and soon the stack grew to about 50 feet long. Our cows loved them and would eat their way into the stack and make a tunnel. Us kids would play hid-and-seek in the tunnels."

Willie: "One year Daddy raised peanuts, and since they were not worth much on the market, he baled them. I spent a lot of time in the barn loft eating peanuts (they were sticking out of the bales) and gained some weight eating them. They were those little Spanish peanuts and tasted so good, yum!

"I used to help Dad grind corn into meal, and I remember the Corn-Sheller we had. It had a hand crank on it, and I had to struggle to turn it, but I turned all I could, and helped put the ears of corn in the top of it. The grist-mill had a gasoline engine to run it, and boy it made a lot of racket. I thought it was going to fly apart any minute, but somehow it stayed together. People from all around brought their corn to get it ground, and Dad would take part of the corn for payment. We had all the corn meal we could eat, and then some."

Note: Our Dad was a country fiddler. When he married Mama, he taught her to play enough chords on the guitar to *second* behind him when he played the fiddle. They were sought after for furnishing music for the country parties, square dances etc. which occurred on weekends.

My brother, Max, wrote a song about our parents: *The Best Two Musicians in Town.* They were indeed the best of their day, and afforded much pleasure for their neighbors because there was no other means for folks to have music unless there were musically talented people among them to play instruments. That was in their earlier years of marriage when they only had two children.

Willie: "Mama and Dad used to play for square dances around the country, and Mama had an old guitar. She knew three chords and showed them to me and I started out on the road to fame. I would play so long that my fingers would get blisters on the ends and I would get so mad that I wanted to bust the guitar over the bed post. I never did do that and worked at it until I got where I could *second* behind somebody. Of course, that made me what I am today."

Edna: "I remember Willie learning to play the guitar, I followed him around...even out to the barn hay loft where Mama made him go to practice! He eventually taught me the chords Mama taught him, and I could sing every song I knew with those three simple chords. Willie did become a fine musician and plays the guitar beautifully. I more or less stayed with three chords...."

Willie: "One last item about Oklahoma: When I was 4

years old, one day on Christmas Eve, I heard some hammering out in the shop. I decided I had better go and check it out. When I got about halfway there, Dad yelled at me and told me to get back to the house. I figured I had done something really bad, so the rest of the day, I stayed hid out.

"When we sat down to supper, Dad didn't seem mad or anything, but I was still real quiet. The next morning, I got up as early as I could and dashed into the living room where the Christmas tree was. There under the tree was the most beautiful stick horse you have ever seen. He had a real horse's head, with real reins, and painted red and white, and had little wheels on the other end. I grabbed him and took him out for a test run. Boy, he was a mighty steed, and could run like the wind. I think I slept with him for a long time."

Note: Daddy could do many things which took skill and ingenuity. In older age when he was retired from regular work, for awhile he occupied himself with making a few pieces of furniture: mostly lamp tables and book cases etc. When we bought an older piano which didn't have a bench, Daddy made one for me! Long ago the piano was replaced with a newer model, but the bench Daddy made remains in my family. It reminds me of how skilled he was in making things.

Mama was skillful in the realm of sewing, making many of our dresses and other things from flour sacks, which were made of printed cloth. The country women of that day depended on the fabric of the flour sacks and since it took two sacks for a dress, the men were instructed to buy two sacks alike! It was a kind public service because of hard times, but it was also a good selling factor for those companies. Two sacks had to be purchased at the same time to get enough for a dress.

Mama also did all of her sewing on a treadle sewing machine. There was no electricity in our part of the county in those days.

Daddy was the one who made our new cotton sacks every fall. I can still see his big feet rocking back and forth on the treadle as he sewed the long sides and ends. He added a few inches each year according to how we had grown. I remember feeling a little important because Daddy made my sack a little longer.

A summer time ritual that I loved was *watermelon time*! Daddy would bring home a big long watermelon. He'd set it on the porch and cut it in long wedges. We each got a piece and we would stand in the yard and eat so we could spit the seeds on the ground. We also had juice dripping from our elbows and chins. We didn't think of using forks. I was near grown before I knew that watermelon was served some other way!

My brother, Jack, has the most vivid memories and some are significant . One such memory has a special *addition* to it. As he was in Germany in peacetime serving a term in the United States Army, he met a native of that country who had memories that connected to our part of the country at that time.

Jack: "A lot happened while we lived on the Little's Place. It was during World War II. I remember an Army truck loaded with German prisoners coming by.

"While stationed in Germany I met a German citizen working on the army post where I was stationed who asked where I was from in the USA. I said Dallas, Texas and he said *'Are you really from Dallas or some other town?'* I said I was really from Clarksville, Texas. He said *'That's just across the river from Idabel, Oklahoma isn't it?'* I said 'Yes, how did you know?' He said he was a prisoner of war stationed at Camp Maxie near Paris, Texas. I told him that I had two questions to ask. 'Were they mean to you and what did you have to eat?' He said that they were very kind and that he ate Post Toasties twice a day. That was what we had to eat and a lot of times we ate them twice a day.....''

Note: Dan, oldest of *the younger ones* had a creative mind and came up with unique ideas. In raising seven sons, Daddy did have the experience of being one of seven sons himself. His mother died when he was young and he helped care for several younger brothers. So he knew boys. He was firm in discipline but fair. I'm sure even Daddy was amazed at the things his boys thought of to do. Dan remembers one of his *inventions* in his early teens that Daddy, for some reason, would not allow.

Dan: "I came by an eight horse power washing machine motor, the old outside ringer type washing machine. I conceived the idea to build a helicopter and fly to school. The first concern was the main rotor. I set up a test to check the motor's power. I built a six foot high stand, hoisted the motor up there and bolted it down with a pulley sticking over the edge. Then I took a 10 foot long 1'x2' board and wired it to the pulley, using figure eight looping of bailing wire. This testing station was in the middle of the driveway of our house. I started the motor. It had just enough power to turn the 10 foot prop at about 100 rpm.

"Daddy came home from work. He stopped the pickup at the entrance of the driveway and stared at me through the windshield of the pickup sitting on top of the test stand beside the motor watching the prop beat the air. He got out of the truck and shouted above the noise of the contraption. *'What are you doing?'* Daddy was always fair about that. He never jumped to the conclusion that you were doing something stupid. He would ask, just to make sure. I cupped my hand around my mouth and shouted back: 'I'm building a helicopter to fly to school!' *'No you're not!'* he said, *'You'll kill your silly self.'* He pulled my permit."

Note: Dan and John were in the birth order to be paired together according to their ages, and so they had their own unique experiences along the way. Many families would go *out West* to pull bolls in the cotton country after the farming season. That gave them extra income for winter. On one such occasion, Daddy took the family and left Dan and John at home to take care of the livestock and watch the place. In writing to Dan in an email conversation, John relates the details of their adventure.

John: "I remember when Daddy and Mama and all the other kids went to pull bolls and we stayed home for two weeks to take care of the livestock. Mother made up a lot of food for us. Daddy said if anyone came around at night to steal stuff just to shoot them. One evening we heard someone in the blacksmith shop and you took the 22 rifle and put a shot through the shop door. Whoever it was came out of there and left a piece of blue jeans on the barbed wire fence and leveled a row of corn all the way to the road next to the Hemingway's.

"I remember going to Amarillo with Neecie and Jack. They lived in some apartments called Tech Village. There were some bullies who beat up on James and Walter and the need for some equal meanness was urgent. Dan and I went and stayed for two weeks. We had fun, though I don't think the bullies enjoyed our stay."

Note: It would take a much larger volume to contain all the memories of the ten Holt children. My aim is merely to show in a few memories of my siblings what life was like for our family back in a forgotten era. Besides the longer narratives of the older ones, I'm sharing a few episodes of memories from each one of the other siblings. Their view of life in their younger years, especially, is most interesting.

Frank: "I rode with Daddy one day, about 1953, into Clarksville to get two big sacks of corn ground up into meal. Riding along in town past all those houses built right next to each other, I remember thinking: *'how do these people get their food; there is no room for their fields.'* I thought the only thing that required money was candy and cokes; for all the other things Daddy always signed a small book at Dinks Store."

Frank: "We raised almost everything we ate. Daddy made *sugar pies* and sent pieces of sugar-cured ham with us to school for lunch. We would trade the sugar pies and the ham to the city kids for baloney sandwiches made with store bought white bread.

"I remember when Mama would make *light bread buns*. It was always a special time with the smell of the yeast bread baking in the oven. It seemed she would bake several big pans on that day and would make us stay out of the kitchen as we would not make the bread *fall*. I never understood what that meant until years later. Eating cornbread almost daily, we always looked forward to *light bread buns* and made short work of them."

Mack: "I don't have farm memories of Neecie and Willie because they were gone from home when we were there. I remember thinking that Edna and Jack were the smartest sister and brother in the world. They were older and seemed to know EVERYTHING! They solved a lot of problems before Mama and Daddy had to get involved. Of course Louis came and took Edna away. My earliest other memory of Louis was when Mama asked him to kill a chicken for dinner. I think he took a 22 caliber rifle and killed that chicken with one shot! I thought, *'No wonder he didn't get killed in the war!'*

"One day in the field I remember Jack getting mad at us because we were not working fast enough. Seems he had a date with Dora and Daddy said he couldn't go until the job was finished. I thought making all that fuss over a girl was the dumbest thing. Boy did I learn my lesson later!

"Sometime later I was with the family out pulling cotton, for some other farmer, I think. (*Pulling* cotton is when you pull the whole boll off the stalk, with the cotton in it. *Picking* cotton is when you *pick* the cotton out of the boll, leaving the boll on the stalk.) I remember that for dinner (lunch for you city folks) Daddy had bought Pickle Loaf and crackers and mustard for us. Frank and I were small enough to sit under the cotton wagon and eat in the shade. I remember how great that meat tasted, (it is still my favorite luncheon meat today.) While we were eating Frank said, *"You know, there are some people who can't afford food like this."* That comment was a surprise to me and I said, "Well, why don't we give them some of ours?" Frank thought for a moment and said, *"We could, if we knew who they were."*

"About a year later I got to know Neecie a little better when she and her husband, Jack Adams, brought the kids for a visit to the farm. Our cousins needed a lot of help; they didn't know anything about the farm. I thought Walter was trying to kill himself when he got a coffee cup from the kitchen and crawled under our meanest cow and tried to milk her! I think that visit was the first time I began to understand what relatives were."

Note: My youngest sister, Connie, was no doubt pampered by Daddy and Mama because she was their baby girl of their older age. She was favored at times, and the boys would scheme to take advantage of it. Such was the case of the *bicycle sale*.

Connie: "Daddy would always give me a dime, but he only gave the boys nickels. I guess being the baby girl, I was special! The boys always were thinking up ways to get me to trade my dime for one of their nickels. One day they came up with a plan! They had gotten an old bicycle somewhere and cleaned it up so they could take turns riding it. The problem was, it had no brakes! They would just let it slow down before hopping off, so the brake problem wasn't an issue, for *them*.

"But one day, they *sold* me the bicycle for one of my dimes. Boy was I excited! They put me on it, and I proudly sped across the yard, with my hair blowing in the wind. It was an exciting experience, *until* I discovered I couldn't get it to stop! In panic I turned into the back yard and went under the clothes line, catching it right in the neck! Ouch!

"Well, the bike finally stopped, but I was on the ground crying and Mama came running to the rescue. The memory of what happened to the boys is a blur, but I am sure Mama told Daddy. One of the boys who sold me the bike might like to share the rest of that memory, then again, maybe not!"

Edna: Our brother, Bruce, was *uncle* to several nephews who were in his age bracket. Willie's son, Mike, recalls the fun they had on a cold 17 degree day when they were about 10 or 11 years old. He relates that Willie and his two sons rode bicycles over to Daddy and Mama's place, picked up Bruce, on his bicycle, and they all took a long ride on one of the coldest days of the winter! When they returned they came back to Willie's and drank hot chocolate to warm up while relishing the experience of the long, cold ride. I'm grateful to Mike for sharing the memory.

PART II

MISCELLANEOUS POEMS

BITS AND PIECES

Our hearts are seldom tidy
In the most that I've known yet.
The are hoarding, sorting, storing
All of life, the worst and best.

Time keeps shoring up the bins
Of thoughts and feelings myriad:
An ample store of pondering,
Vivid heart imprints life has made.

Hearts fill to seeming capacity
With fragments lingering intently about:
Bits and pieces of lasting impressions
Often yearning to venture out.

Some disguise, eluding detection.
Others are open, revealing a part.
Such are random bits and pieces
From the holdings of my heart.

WORDS

In the night they came: eager, alert,
Scrambling into formation;
Jostling each other for position;
Boisterous;

Equipped with hidden meaning,
And emotion.
Fickle too...not waiting;
Dawn came. They were gone.

PREFERENCE

I'd prefer a fine book to a diamond,
Though it sparkle with a tempting gleam.
Valuable thought in words far outlast
The worth of a tantalizing gem.

But sell the diamond, buy many books...
Is said with condescending disdain
As though I'm slow to comprehend
The merit of a jewel's possession.

The luster may weaken the bent of my soul,
And set a craving to disquiet me within.
My price is far above rubies and diamonds
Whether they ever cross my hand.

Books that feed contentment,
Or whet the yearning to be...and know,
Increase one's durable riches
Beyond comparison of mere polished stones.

A PATCH OF BLUE

In the heaps of childhood memories,
Occasionally showing through,
I see the old pitcher on the table:
A pretty patch of blue.

It was ordinary and useful
With its soothing, restful hue.
Adding color in my childhood frame:
A pretty patch of blue.

THE LADY

Occasionally since I was a little girl,
I've caught a glimpse of her in others.
It's always an impressive moment,
When suddenly we're close to one another.

After I'd grown and had a family,
I'd see her; she'd appear suddenly,
Always in a familiar place for me
To see, and I'd admire her greatly.

Years passed. Then I chanced to see
Her driving by one day, unexpectedly.
She gave a polite nod in my direction.
How perfectly serene her life must be.

Now in middle age I've wondered,
And just today the answer came.
While I was choosing out some apples,
She came walking by again.

I stopped to gaze admiringly,
Her perfection hasn't diminished at all.
I always know her, though she doesn't know me:
The lady I've always wanted to be.

THREE LOOKS

The old fellow chortled with plain delight
For the circumstance, though sad as could be,
Had caused his dear wife to cling to him,
Her hero again after decades on end,
And the old fellow told it with obvious glee
While she looked at him in proper lady accord
With expression that has no adequate words.

In the back of the church one Sunday morn,
The deacon rose in 'word of testimony' time.
He rambled on in his sincerest tone
Speaking of love in subtle comparison,
Eloquently impressing others and himself utmost.
He finished, sinking down in the pew until set,
While a thoughtful sideways look from his wife
Is an expression words haven't been made for yet.

She came down the aisle that day at last,
A vision in white satin, ruffles, and lace.
Filmy illusion fell from snowy brim
Veiling the bride's radiant smiling face.
It was that once in a lifetime scene
For the groom, looking steadfastly at his bride.
He guided her gently to their place to vow.
We observed the wonder...the look in his eyes,
But lack fitting words that look to describe.

PEASANT GIRL

She had a longing, incredibly sad look,
Gazing across barriers others can't see:
Time and chance, customs and place,
And possessions that would never be.

The windows of her very soul
Look further than tangibles here.
In their depth is full awareness of truth
Matured with a life of hardship and care.

She cradles in her peasant arms
Long sheaves of green and brown,
Foliage to arrange in her cottage room
Like she'd seen in the village town.

Probing life's depths, wondering,
She'd often met looks of disdain.
It matters not; her heart is resigned.
She hugs the sheaves and turns homeward again.

Such haunting beauty attracted each day,
An image the mind would often recall.
We left her enshrined in loneliness
In the picture on the wall.

THE WELL

The street used to be the first road
From country to town so they tell.
It threaded its way by the wooded yard
Of the home-place owning the well.

Decades of local travelers
During the heat of summer days,
Stopped by for a drink of water
At the well nestled in the shade.

It furnished many a comfort
For neighbors, or passer-by.
The well offered more than water,
It nourished a way of life.

The years passed; progress developed.
New replaced old in the deal.
Now a house depicting no character
Sets nearby claiming the well.

They decided to leave it standing,
Since it stood off out of the way.
The top was sealed...flowers planted;
The well had 'passed' its day.

It's sad that an era has ended.
Folks would linger with news to tell
Around something with trustworthy dignity,
Such as the old time-marked well.

Note: I have always loved the history of old houses. I enjoy going through them and imagining what it was like with people living there, and how the house looked in its original time period. One day we passed one such old house on the highway. My heart was moved when I saw a vulture perched on the chimney as though the old house was weak and dying.

THE HOUSE

It was admirable to behold...
The old house tenaciously standing
As it had through generations before,
But now so near dilapidation.

How could folks have deserted
The house with its broad friendly face?
Surely decades of living and loving entwined
Sowed richness and memories in the place.

The house depicts dignity in rejection,
For perhaps a modern design somewhere.
Its character is prevalent, though quite alone,
Except for its trees stripped winter-bare.

Motionless, a vulture perched on the chimney
As though it sensed and patiently waited
For the old house to give up...decease,
As its life ebbed away in decaying.

Note: I visited our elderly members who were residents in the Nursing Homes in the days of our pastorate. For some it was temporary but for others it was their last home. I learned from those *children of yesterday* as I tried to encourage them, listen to their stories, and offer comfort and hope from the sure promises of God's Word.

WAITING...

We are waiting for our conveyance...

The confident tone,
And slight lift of her chin
Bespoke of other years:
Times of respect and commanding.

Experience and knowledge,
Enough to enrich a whole generation,
Is stored irretrievably
In these children of yesterday.

Living in a maze of confused memories
And fanciful dreams, they wander about
In their world touching others
Who share their redesigned existence.

And they are waiting...all waiting
For their conveyance,
Which will come someday
And quietly take them away.

THE RESIDENT

She was seated near a window, savoring sunshine
Pouring over frail shoulders bundled in a sweater.
"I'm always cold." She said quietly.

We talked of long ago, of childhood, youth
And special skills learned early
In her time frame.

She recalled piecing a colorful Star quilt,
Relating with obvious pleasure
That, even now, it covers her bed.

A girlish smile attended the pleasant memory
Of courtship, and the young suitor
Who succeeded in blending
Her destiny with his own.

Such memories span eight decades of time:
A unique treasure guarded with dignity
And repose in a slight frame.
She spoke softly, "I'm so glad you came."

Outside the air was crisp and cool.
I drove away stirred with desire, as usual,
To set words to the music of her life.

I could imagine her tottery journey
Down the hallway to the room at the end...
The door ajar, I glimpsed bright colors
Of a tangible bit of the past.

She sleeps...warmed by fond memories,
Under her enduring bright stars.

Note: Fall is the most wonderful season the Lord made! At least it is to me. I've always loved it, even as a child. It is probably because I liked school so well and fall was the time that the school year began. When I was five years old, and my older sister and brother went off to the schoolhouse just a stone's throw from our house, I was devastated because I couldn't go.

One morning I decided to sneak out through our corn field, which was very near the schoolhouse, and just show up when the bell rang for starting time. After everyone was inside, I cracked the door open and smiled as far as my mouth would stretch when the teacher looked at me, hoping she would be impressed and let me stay. Well that lovely lady smiled back! At that time I thought she must have a hundred teeth...all sparkly white. Wonder of wonders! She allowed me to sit in the row with her first grade students, gave me a paper with a grid of one hundred blocks drawn on it and showed me how to make numbers.

Then I couldn't stay away. I came each day...a few minutes after starting time, and did my smiling act. She allowed me to stay because, unknown to me, she consulted with my parents. My Dad being on the school board of that country school might have helped the case, and she kindly took me in since I was interrupting every morning just as she started teaching. The schoolhouse had two big rooms, each containing six grades. To me it was a citadel of knowledge. I learned to write my numbers to one hundred on that grid, and started reading in the *See Spot...See Spot Run* books for beginners.

Within two years we moved. A wagon pulled by a team of horses was our *moving van.* I remember feeling sad as I watched the schoolhouse slowly recede from my view as we lumbered past it. There I had gotten my first taste of *book-learning,* which set the love of books and search for knowledge in my heart. I never excelled in math as I did other subjects, but I can, to this day, write the numbers from one to a hundred on a grid with 100 little squares!

BLEAK OF A WINTER DAY

In the bleak of a cold winter day,
The school yard empty from holidays,
The child wandered in contented leisure
Feeling the awe and wonder of the place.

Toeing deliberate impressions in the sand,
Listening to wind swish in the pine trees,
She wondered if treasures might be hidden near
By fairies, or pirates, or the teacher this year.

The treasures inside, she knew very well:
Books for numbers, reading, and singing:
Blackboards and chalk, other things to excite;
Even a bell for recess ringing.

Suddenly, she saw with a gasp of delight
A sparkle like diamonds in the sunlight.
Where the Christmas tree was thrown down,
Bits of tinsel were scattered in the sand.

Stooping, she examined the shining treasure,
Fancying the horde all at once on the tree.
She stirred tiny sparkles in sand with her finger
In that moment of richness for memory.

She left it all on the cold moist ground,
To perish in wind and weather.
The valuable was taken along on her way:
Contentment alone on a cold winter day.

FALL

Some folks favor springtime,
Or summer's frivolous days;
But fall is the season
Excelling in every way.

It's the most thoughtful season,
Relieving summer's heat.
Also famous for learning,
Labeled 'school days', it's replete.

Fall stirs up many desires
To baking, fixing, planning...
Invigorated by crisp coolness
Of days too brief in lasting.

Fall is an emotional season,
Trembling...swirling...changing,
Causing restless thoughts and sighs
Like an extraordinary lovely painting.

We are treated to the spectacle
Of fall's colossal show:
Blending awesome array of colors
So skillfully one can't know.

Constantly rearranging its scenes
Of both subtle and brilliant foliage,
Until stripped of all, fall slips away
Into mysterious winter storage.

We wait and anticipate another year,
As fall primps just right
To make its annual debut;
For it always...always comes back.

A HINT OF FALL

It's lurking about, almost teasing,
Supposing to draw me away
From the dwindling days of summer
Wearing weariness now on its face.

A few dried leaves drifted slowly down
On the path I walked today.
My heart leaped in anticipation!
It's close, though still hidden away.

Fall shall hold us fast in its spell;
Willing captives, as usual, we'll be
Of this illustrious season
Coloring days beautiful with incredible ease.

THE EARLY SNOW

Quietly it came down, laying a soft
White blanket over the brilliance of fall.
The wind became motionless, and serenely silent
Amidst softly swirling snowflakes.
Sparse golden leaves shivered as the feathery coldness
Clung to branches of their trees.

Sturdy flowers bowed bright faces for shelter.
Rustic brown fallen leaves ceased their jittery
Little swirls on the ground.
Soon picturesque fall lay stunned
Beneath the icy splendor...waiting.
Just so quickly it melted away.
The early snow.

LATE AUTUMN RAIN

Distant thunder rumbles, wind is blowing
Swirling leaves across the ground.
Colors are not as varied now,
Hues are shades of gold and brown.

A few tenacious ones are clinging
To branches of the trees,
But the gentle sprinkling of today's rain
Trembles them fearfully.

Autumn is starting a grand decline,
Yet stealing nature's show;
The full moon peeped through last night,
Limbs hung with leaves of gold.

Yellow pansies with drooping eyes
Lean close to coppery mums,
Watching restlessly in the rain
Knowing winter must come.

The wonder of color in autumn
We can never ascertain.
The Creator isn't sparing with beauty.
He has countless autumns we've never seen.

CROW ON A FENCE

He was strictly not worried you could see,
As he surveyed the field leisurely.
In a quick comparison easily made
Of creature advantages, mine are high.
But he can fly.

Of course I know, for I have read
The exhortation, 'take no thought for your life',
But sitting calmly is that fowl of the air:
A feathery example and gently rebuke. I sigh.
And he can fly.

A creature not tired or the least flustered
From a frantic search for food or things,
Or concerned at all of tomorrow's plight;
He just perched for a moment, then took to flight.
For he can fly.

ON GROWING OLDER

Time is galloping at breakneck speed
Like a wild runaway horse, pulling us along
Hollering "whoa!" But there's no heed;
It's bent on running, swifter as it goes.

Aren't we wise and mature enough
To appreciate the years, their experience?
We are...and we are not.
Our hearts flip in and out of contentment.

We acknowledge birthdays, atop our heap of years
Streaked with gold and silver shining:
Memories that bind us to them...all our days.

FRIEND

Our first meeting was in youthful days
Of unlined face...of physical vim
When life was hardly yet troublesome;
Not having that measure of capacity
For her...or for me, but I could sense
That she would be my friend.

Maturity unfolded, revealing responsibility
Of family, work, troubles, sorrows,
And the peculiar suffering of the living
Over the dying...and the dead.
I've stood by her side; she has stood by mine
Gently squeezing my hand: An understanding friend.

The storm winds came and stirred her life:
Fierce, raging, unusually rife.
Yet she was not driven from the way,
And through the years I have thoughtfully
And prayerfully regarded my friend.

Now age is visible on her face...and mine.
Decades have drifted by like 0sand,
And life persists in taking by subtle force
The quiet happiness we all yearn for at sunset.

But wisdom has prevailed over youth.
A seasoned patience has grown out of trials
And her faith is entrenched in her heart,
Making calm in the midst of 'all things'.
Such is a treasure...a special friend.

Note: I stood by the old barn that was half way fallen to the ground, and wondered at the small size of it; I remembered it being so huge when I was a child. I'd chased the bumblebees there and we ran Mama's ducks through the hallway. Mama had made Willie bring his first guitar to the hay-loft to practice. Yes, I went back...but nothing seemed familiar anymore.

GOING BACK

"You can't go back" you've heard it said.
Some determine to go anyway.
So, carefully, I traveled that aged road
We had walked as children, just yesterday.

The way had shortened considerably,
Several miles I'd say.
How surprising...I remember that old road;
It stretched on forever, winter through May.

I lingered at the place
Where our house and fence had stood.
The old barn alone remained,
Shrunken now, a heap of decaying wood.

Even the trees whose awesome size
Thrilled my childish heart and dreams,
Had somehow shriveled and cowered down
Through decades of changing seasons.

I didn't believe you couldn't go back,
And went just to look and linger.
The past gave no hint of knowing at all;
I stood there...a total stranger.

IN MY PLACE

They developed the habit early in life,
By the time school was their chore,
Arriving in the evening of the day
Hollering "Mama!" as they entered the door.

A word of my presence was all they desired,
Whether inside or just around.
Things were all right with 'mother' about;
"Mama!"...I can still hear the sound.

I've made many mistakes at least
In the heat of this mother's race;
But when my children were young
And called "Mama!"...

I was always in my place.

HOME IS WHERE THE HEART IS

Yes, it's there, but at times you have to look.
It may be buried under laundry,
Floating in gooey dishwater,
Or cringing in a corner dreading housework.

It's there, at times wounded by unkind words
Then gladdened by a touch or smile.
A little hug completes its happiness;
The heart loves home and thrives there.

Home is where the heart is,
Helping love weave its unique spell
Of happiness, contentment, and belonging.
Without it, home is an empty shell.

TO A YOUNG GIRL

You have a Friend who is present,
With your every step a part;
Not by your side to see with eyes,
But securely in your heart.

He offers great encouragement
With present help from His word.
"I think of you all the time." He says;
And you can believe the Lord!

No one cares so very much
How you feel, look...or if you cry.
The Lord has proven it ever so much;
He had you in His heart when He died.

So walk with His presence every day,
And quietly acknowledge Him there.
He will be pleased and delight in your love.
You've got the dearest Friend, who cares.

TO A NEW FRIEND

We could have passed by on the street,
And only exchanged a smile or nod.
Polite folk may know hundreds that way,
Though not one, perhaps, as they would.

But destiny designed a little wonder,
And our life circles overlapped.
Perchance the Lord smiled and nodded...
Anyway, I have found you out.

GRANDMOTHER BELLE

Was she tall? Yes, and so graceful,
Or maybe she just looked that way
To a wee little girl my mother was
In those wonderful long ago days

When her *Mama* was there...sweet memories
Cut off at the age of nine,
When suddenly, it was a common tragedy,
Belle and a new baby died.

After that life was hard
For a little girl not yet ten.
How do you fill up the awesome space
Where a mother's love has been?

But she grew up tenacious of life
With talents that amaze us still.
She loved to read books though she had few,
And she was musically inclined as well.

In Mother's life someone made a print,
Carefully done, early, and well.
The traits passed down can't be explained
Unless they came from Grandmother Belle.

Note: My grandmothers, **Perneecie Mills Holt** and **Belvie Ann Eason Roberts** were born in the 1800's. I never saw them for they died when my parents were children. Not every mother gets the opportunity of enjoying *grandmother-hood.* I'm thankful for the privilege in my life of being a grandmother and great grandmother.

Note: One fall at the opening week of Bible College, we were there and a young lady from our church, the dorm supervisor, invited me to have the evening devotions with the girls. They all gathered in one room, sitting around the bunks and floor chattering with excitement.

I thought to encourage them by mentioning that hundreds of young men right here on the campus were unattached; *"acres and acres"* I said as they began shaking their heads in disagreement. I said "Well, my son is up here...." to which a hand raised quickly and a voice said as matter-of-fact, *"He's taken!"* And that is the way I first heard that a lovely girl with shiny hair cascading down to her waist had captured our son's attention and heart. It would be permanent.

TO JAN

We first saw you in springtime,
Possessing such youthful beauty and grace,
It had already captured our son's attention and heart.

Through the struggle of beginnings
You made a home within the house,
And remained sweet in spirit
As life, at times, dealt vicious blows against
The walls enclosing your happiness and tranquility.

You patiently watched the pitter-pattering of little feet
On through the various stages children pass through,
Even enduring adolescence whose turbulence
Mercifully subsides, somehow, before adulthood.

Now you are absorbing the bittersweet reality
Of your offspring being grown,
And the inevitable future which holds springtime...

God always gives more than we deserve
For which we acknowledge and gratefully praise Him.
Within our family circle...*He placed you.*

BLOOM WHERE YOU ARE PLANTED

It may be the back of a desert,
The middle of a swamp or marsh;
Or a barren, scraggly prairie
Where breath is stifled by dust.
Life is a unique garden:
Briars and thorns among delicate things.
It molds us character and patience
As we're torn, stuck, and soothed again.

Are you planted in a desert place
Or wading a murky swamp?
Perhaps you're struggling for fresh air
In the plot holding you just now.
Look up, and out of the tangled growth
To One who adds fragrance and hue.
Open your heart, let petals unfold,
And where you are planted...bloom.

THE PARTING OF YOUTH

There was relief and also comfort
In facing the insistent truth,
And accepting the age-old challenge
To release my eager youth.
Companions we were for decades of time,
Perfectly compatible in rhythm and rhyme.
But youth grew impatient of my slower pace
As years became hurdles in life's daily race.
The time came...she quietly withdrew
At the place where make-believe stops.
I won't try to call her back;
Or pretend youth is here when she's not.

SHARING

I started to share some memories of service
With a young friend today...
The times I used to do this or that.
I expected a response of interest,
Even a polite one, but there was none.

After our years have accumulated
Like mountains of debris,
Why do we long to search through them
For bits and pieces of things others will value?
Only You understand and can satisfy
Every longing of the heart.
Thank You, Lord.

A TIME TO SOW

Marriage is a very good field
In which to sow the good things...
Seeds of love, kindness, respect, courtesy
And forgiveness.

Make up your own little bundle
Of 'happiness seeds'
And start sowing and watering
On your side of the fence.

The grass will always be greener there,
Instead of on the other side.
There is no margin for error;
We do reap what we sow...

MOTHERS...A HEARTY LOT

You are burden-bearers: you carry
Your unborn for months, then ever after
As they travel the road of life.

First, your arms are full...of baby, and *stuff*;
For mothers must be prepared for *anything.*

As the children move from your arms onto the
Path of growing up, and toward maturity,
They load up your heart; and you carry
Their concerns and problems...lightened
Perhaps by prayer, but never quite gone.

You can love, and do love your offspring
In and through every circumstance...
Sometimes to the wonder of all!

The light of your love never goes out,
Or even flickers, in the winds
Of heartaches and disappointments.

Toward the evening of life
Your title becomes *Grand...*
And children of your children snuggle
Into your heart as well, confident
And secure in your love.

Mothers...you are that vital part
In the cycle of life, and we salute you!

You Are A Hearty Lot.

MY PART

God's peculiar treasure on earth,
Those precious souls redeemed,
At times may fill a vital place
And become our own...it seems.

I clung tenaciously as a child
Holding tight another's things.
Mine! My heart cried stubbornly,
As the Lord gently pried open my hands.

They are mine, He quietly reminded.
Release them, it's for the best.
I decide where my jewels shall sparkle;
They are not yours to possess.

My tears fell on empty hands,
As peace flooded my heart.
Desire for God's will sprang anew:
Tending the treasure, again my part.

THE GOD-CALLED PREACHER

Who can describe that inward bent,
The call of God on the man He's sent?
He lives and serves in the Lord's design,
Not a shallow thing such as 'change of mind.'

Like a mighty oak of many generations,
A long-time preacher is a prized creation.
With roots grown deep in strength of the Lord,
He understands the power of the Word.

As the body grows older, not heart and mind,
God's call stays vibrant, ageless in time.
Decades of dedicated service commend
The God-called preacher, faithful to the end.

POEMS

THAT

SPRANG

FROM

A

VERSE

SEASONS

We plod through endless seasons,
The ups and downs of life,
Waiting for that special one:
An end to all the strife.

Fierce battles rage and then dwindle.
Perhaps the end's in sight
In the struggle to keep my heart each day:
A season full of bloom and blight...
That never quite goes away.

The battle is the Lord's
Yet I swing with all my might,
And lose focus in the struggle
Of the season to increase faith and sight.

Patiently He cycles the seasons,
All different and especially designed
To teach us, to grow us, to mold us alike
In His image...in our earthly time.

Romans 8:29

"For whom he did foreknow, he also did predestinate
to be conformed to the image of his Son, that he might be
the firstborn among many brethren."

CONFRONTATION

Not all were mean or spiteful lots:
The memories of my childhood time.
Yet a monster of misery stalked my heart
With never fatigue or decline.

Always observing with greedy eyes,
Fed by my thoughts like a flame.
It consumed the very life of my life,
Ignoring my pleading with disdain.

One day my heart made a desperate stand,
To the death it had to be.
Surprising strength and confidence appeared
As a faint hope stirred in me.

"It's as though you've never been," I cried.
"You're dust and ashes to me.
What ever I am and shall become
Is in God's realm of possibility."

The power of those words was amazing.
With defeat came a despairing cry.
The past dwindled in size before my eyes,
And fell at my feet...and died.

Mark 9:23

"Jesus said unto him, If thou canst believe,
all things are possible to him that believeth."

DO THOU FOR ME

Do Thou for me, Lord.
Help me to recognize and admit my own
Slothful neglect of devotion to You;
To gather my wandering thoughts
As I read your word, and pray;
To make your word a reality in my life:
The song to sing
The sword to swing,
The rock to keep me steady.

Do Thou for her, Lord.
Help her sort out thoughts and feelings
That may be churning in her heart.
Give her reassurance in prayer, renew her hope.
Reveal a new precious promise
To her heart from your word:
A song to sing,
A sword to swing,
A rock to keep her steady.

Psalms 109:21

"But do thou for me, O God the Lord
for thy name's sake."

KEEP THY HEART

Plow it: the soil is naturally hard,
The clods make stumbling stones.
Plow often, keeping the ground soft
And receptive for planting.
The Word is The Plow.
Seed it: sow in the furrows deeply,
Making them fertile beds
For seeds to germinate and grow.
The Word is The Seed.

Water it: pour in that heavenly moisture
Which sustains life; soil and
Seeds thirst for it continually.
The Word is The Water.

Weed it: cut out poisonous things
Which easily flourish, choking
The things growing there.
A sharp sword is the best tool.
The Word is The Sword.

Harvest it: gather, then share
The bounty and beauty
From your well-kept heart.
Keep Thy Heart With All Diligence.

Proverbs 4:23

"Keep thy heart with all diligence:
for out of it are the issues of life."

LOOKING AHEAD

You notice the valleys are deeper
And the mountains seemingly high,
And our steps more plodding with effort
As time rushes crazily by.

Hear the tireless roar of the devourer,
Though toothless and fangless he be.
In the spiritual warfare that's raging,
There's a psychological part you see.

For there is always rattling of the chains,
Though truth has set us free.
It is disquieting to our souls
And renders us fearful, doubting victory.

But there is calm in the eye of the battle
Where conflict ceases to be.
It's a secret place known to few,
Directly at Jesus' feet.

Courage and strength are there reinforced.
Resolve is polished to a sheen.
And love drives out fear and doubt,
Just lingering in that place with Him.

I Peter 5:8

"Be sober, be vigilant; because your
adversary the devil, as a roaring lion,
walketh about, seeking whom he may devour."

THE LORD'S PLACE

The enemy waited with anticipation
To hinder progress in the race.
Confident of my own strength for the day,
I by-passed my visit to the Lord's place.

I'd been triumphant days on end,
And felt no dismay at the start
As the enemy met me in the usual place
Right outside the door of my heart.

They dogged my path relentlessly,
Being bolder with each suggestion.
Turning to wield the sword of strength,
My knees had stiffened; my arms were weak.

And now my eyes seemed faintly dim,
The path of faith blurred to them.
In just a day...how could it be?
In panic I cried, "My Lord, help me!"

A victorious shout pierced the way!
One scarred by divine destiny
Unsheathed His sword with its blinding gleam,
And stepped between the enemy...and me.

One powerful blow put the enemy to flight,
Frantic to avoid that sword!
In the stillness kind words gave strength and resolve:
Get back to the place of the Lord.

I Chronicles 16:27
"Glory and honor are in his presence;
strength and gladness are in his place."

CAST THY BREAD

Bread gleaned by your heart and hand,
With time and determination to gather,
Is rich with promise and strength for the day,
And like the manna, can't be hoarded away.
Cast thy bread...multiplied numbers have never been fed.

Waters may be billowing with roughness,
Or placid as a pool can be.
It matters not, cast as He said;
The bread calms or livens miraculously.
Cast thy bread expectantly...send truth across life's sea.

One finds it at last, the far-flung bread,
Before the Lord bowing in a multitude fed.
After many days, the sure promise said,
Because faithful ones hearkened and cast the bread.
Cast thy bread...you will find, more than cast, multiplied.

Ecclesiastes 11:1

"Cast thy bread upon the waters:
for thou shalt find it after many days."

THE PRISONER

The prison was an imposing thing,
A fortress with massive guarded walls
Kept sure by decades of anguish, frustration,
And pleasure in life's bitter fruition.

A prisoner dwelt securely within,
Who deemed to mar my life...its joys.
He would die there; it seemed his fate.
No other, or I could open the gate.

Locks were rusted with bitterness and hate,
And though many feeble efforts were made
When remorse or compassion stirred the night,
Determination alone could not end the plight.

But oh the wonder of God's grace!
In pity He regarded the weary, the weak.
He placed in my hand a little key
With an able command: *Set the prisoner free.*

A touch of the key swung wide the gate.
The tenant had vanished to freedom's side.
In wonder of truth I gazed at the heap
Of chains unshackled around my feet.

Hebrews 12:15

" Looking diligently lest any man fail of the
grace of God; lest any root of bitterness
springing up trouble you, and thereby
many be defiled."

FRAGMENTS THAT REMAIN

Fragments! That's all I received that night,
Words that pierced with deadly aim.
They lodged in my heart with purpose;
I was saved because fragments remained.

Thousands number the sermons
I've heard with dutiful heart.
They left nuggets of truth in the washing,
The fragments becoming my part.

With so little serious fervor in prayer,
And devoted time to His word,
I've never attained all He has for me,
But only fragments from the dear Lord.

Fellowship sweet with God's children...
Refreshing as needed rain,
Sweet memories lingering sustain me:
Those fragments that remain.

They are the gracious bounty of God
Gathered up for spiritual gain,
For we really can't contain the whole,
But only fragments that remain.

John 6:12

"When they were filled, he said unto his
disciples, Gather up the fragments that
remain, that nothing be lost."

CIRCLE THOUGHTS

Things that bless most are not big and grand,
But uniquely simple, the size of a hand.
Attainable...ordinary...touchable...free,
Stirred by love in my sisters and me.

It may be a smile with a tender look,
An inspiring thought read in a book,
Or a verse the Lord revealed one day:
Little things to sow in special ways.

It could be a sweet thing, big as a cake,
Or a shoulder to cry on when one is weak.
Opportunities have wings, swiftly they go!
Reach out and grasp one; determine to sow.

Galatians 6:10

"As we have therefore opportunity, let us do
good unto all men, especially unto them
who are of the household of faith."

THE HIDDEN CARE

Perhaps the need one cannot see;
Life seems perfect as can be;
Yet lodged in the underneath part,
Is a little care hidden in the heart.
We pray, then, since God does know,
Any and all concealed from show.
His love overturns the underneath part,
And tends the care hidden in the heart.

133

JOY IN THE PRESENCE

Faint words are flung out in a desperate cry
From the sea of humanity toward the throne.
God...be merciful to me...a sinner.
Heaven is transfixed in silence,
Beholding the face of the Savior.
A shadow of identification and love
Reflects in those fathomless eyes.
The Father nods His acceptance.
Heaven bursts forth in rejoicing,
And the angels watch in speechless wonder...
Another soul is redeemed for eternity.

Luke 15:10

"Likewise I say unto you, there is joy in the presence of the
angels over one sinner that repenteth."

WITHOUT ME...NOTHING

Heaps of *nothing* are piled around us.

To our shame, praise of men is such a welcomed sound

To our prideful hearts, that for a display of *nothing,*

We accept acclaim.

Lord help me to see that hoarded collection

Of doings, mine alone, for what it is:

Nothing... designated to be consumed.

I repent now, remembering God's warning:

For without me, ye can do nothing.

John 15:5

".... He that abideth in me, and I in him, the same bringeth
forth much fruit: for without me ye can do nothing."

THE GIFT

Give a gift to Jesus? What does one give to a King

Who has untold treasure, the universe,

And myriad angels who do His bidding?

I'm least among His servants...what could I give?

Yet...there is one thing He desires of mine.

I'm thrilled, but frightened, and tremble at the thought

Of laying such a gift at His feet.

But His love constrains me.

So I take this tattered, rather roughened thing:

Dull with lack of courage,

Shriveled from lack of nourishment,

Slippery with a spidery web of deceit,

And I hold it out to the King...with fear and trembling.

Lord, I present to You this unworthy gift;

I give to You...my heart.

Matthew 2:11

"...and when they had opened their treasures,
they presented unto him gifts;
gold, frankincense, and myrrh."

THE THORN

"Lord, I want it gone." I had said.
For years the thorn had pained me sore
And I insisted to God:
"I don't want this thorn anymore."

There was a heavy, holy silence.
I'd hardly expected an affirmative reply.
Yet little did I know God's working
Was set in motion to relieve my plight.

It's blessed recollecting many things
He miraculously wrought from that day.
I didn't know or really care how,
Just that He'd move it from my way.

At times my impatience would surface.
I'd fret for the burden I'd borne.
"My child"...the Lord spoke so kindly,
"Your foolishness embedded the thorn."

Fearfully I began to understand
What God would have me know,
As He removed the tenacious thing
And there remained a gaping hole.

"Oh Lord" I cried, "How can I survive
Such a terrible wound that's made?"
"My child there's healing and comfort
In my Word...the balm in Gilead

Numbed by agony and desperate need
To have the yawning hole filled in,
The Word grew sweeter to my heart
And more real than it had ever been.

(Continued)

137

The Lord and I had fellowship
So satisfying as never before.
It was worth the pain and agony
Made by the thorn and gaping hole.

One day I remembered the oft request
And brought it timidly again to His throne.
He bade me look on the dreaded thing.
The wound of the thorn was gone.

II Corinthians 12:9
"...My grace is sufficient for thee:..."

UNSEEMLY

A vagrant searched through garbage cans
Along an alley, looking for food...or things.
I pitied him.
My heart went searching, defiantly,
Through the world's garbage and polluted debris
Looking for something to satisfy.
It was so unseemly for a king's child.
All heaven pitied me.

Galatians 4:9

"But now, after that ye have known God, or rather are
known of God, how turn ye again to the weak and beggarly
elements, whereunto ye desire again to be in bondage?"

LET YOUR EYES AFFECT YOUR HEART

It may be an obvious burden
That alters the routine of her days,
Or one that lies hidden in 'unspoken',
Which grieves the heart away.

Or the numbness of depression
That quenches her spirit inside,
Making life a plodding...not a joy,
And senses weary of desperation's cry.

Stand still. Gaze into her valley;
Let your eyes affect your heart,
Until compassion and love make a plea:
"Lord...in Your caring, let me have a part."

Lamentations 3:51

"Mine eye affecteth mine heart
because of all the daughters of my city."

FROM THE WAY

The sparkle was gone from her eyes
Which did radiate such happiness
In days past.Even the dew of dormant tears
Could not imitate it.
How easily we wander from the way
Into the place of sadness and regret.

Psalm 119:176

"I have gone astray like a lost sheep;
Seek thy servant; for I do not forget thy commandments."

TENT PEG

Mute servant, often overlooked,
Clinging to its designated place in the ground;
Never a part of the striking silhouette at sunset
But there nevertheless:
Fastened to, and affecting the destiny of the whole:
Small, hammered down, stumbled over, unnoticed:
A tent peg.

A seemly counterpart: my frail tent.
Driven deep into the Foundation,
Fastened securely in His will and purpose,
Holding steady while storms blow,
Straining ropes anchoring my life
With its hopes and desires toward God...

One stands:
Small, hammered down, stumbled over, unnoticed:
A tent peg.

I Thessalonians 1:3

"Remembering without ceasing your work
of faith, and labour of love, and patience of
hope in our Lord Jesus Christ....."

PRAYER THOUGHT

(Inspired by a friend)

Rain...attending duty, commitment and love
Can make such a lot of mud.
Lord, I feel so tired...and dirty
From wading in this muck.

I'm lifting up my eyes, Lord, gazing intently
To glimpse your face daily;
It must be daily...hourly...each minute.

Lead me in a plain path, Lord,
You know where I must step.
All I see is fearful bog
Threatening to pull me under.

Will the flowers ever grow here, Lord?
I've planted, tended, worked this garden
And my sweat and tears testify.

But rain is unrelenting, not gentle, but hard
And I wait...trusting You for the future
That, thankfully, I cannot see.

Psalm 138:7

"Though I walk in the midst of trouble,
thou wilt revive me..."

THINKING OF YOU

It's a comforting message from His Word,
As things go right...or wrong.
Molehill troubles turn to mountains, yet,
"I think toward you..." says the Lord.

My heart was full, silently pleading;
You passed by too distracted to see
One longing for a touch, or smile.
The moment passed...do you think of me?

I meant to call, but was busy that day;
Other opportunities slipped away.
Coldness soon pierced me like a sword,
And I ran cringing to God's Word,
Was warmed by His love...and thought of you.

Jeremiah 29:11

"For I know the thoughts that I think
toward you, saith the Lord..."

ARE YOU PLANTED

Are you planted...
Your roots growing toward, seeking out,
And desperately desiring the water?

Are you planted...
Swaying in fierce winds of adversity,
Thrashed about in storms of life,
Yet clinging to the soil determined to survive?

Are you planted...
Notched by the axe for destruction;
Yet sending roots deeper,
As healing tears close the wound,
Though the scar remains?

Are you planted...
Gnarled, bent, and roughened by time;
But laden with fruit,
Sweetened with maturity?

Are you planted?

Psalm 92:13-14

"Those that be planted in the house of the Lord
shall flourish in the courts of our God.
they shall still bring forth fruit in old age;
they shall be fat and flourishing..."

CEASE FROM STRIFE

Girding on my sword,
I sought the familiar battlefield where the enemy
Lurked in the shadows
Anticipating the delight of dancing about
Just out of reach of my slashing sword
Of anger and frustration.

The day ended as usual.
Homeward I trudged, weary with fatigue,
Helpless to quell the hurt of another battle lost,
While the enemy scampered back into the
Comfortable recesses of my mind
To await another day.

Then You showed me Your sword: sharp,
Two-edged, gleaming from countless victories.
It pierced my heart
Cutting cleanly into the wound for healing,
Then with a blow destroyed the enemy,
Leaving a settled peace.

Thank You, Lord.

Proverbs 20:3

"It is an honor for a man to cease from strife..."

LEGACY

We are leaving a sure legacy
On the path of life we trod.
Is it treasure of the precious kind
Reminding others of our God?

The legacy that points to God,
A pattern of will and obedient design,
Is beyond wealth gleaned from the earth,
Which cankers and rusts with time.

Make clear impressions in sands of time,
Footprints of love and faith that's deep.
Others following in your wake
Will have a legacy to keep.

Proverbs 4:26-27

"Ponder the path of thy feet,
and let all thy ways be established.
Turn not to the right hand nor to the left:
remove thy foot from evil."

TWAS THE TIME BEFORE CHRISTMAS

Twas the time before Christmas
And all through the earth
Hardly any expected the dear Savior's birth.

The prophets of God in centuries gone by
Had foretold His birth with many a sigh,

For they longed to see this wonder to be,
Yet they passed from the scenes of history.

Then one day, as quiet as the dawn
The angel told a virgin, "You will have a son."

In the fullness of time by God's holy decree
Christ came to earth from eternity.

The angels came down to proclaim!
The shepherds hurried to worship Him.
The baby they gazed at in wonder that night
Changed the world
From the time before Christmas.

Luke 2:11

"For unto you is born this day in the city of David
a Saviour, which is Christ the Lord."

TRIBUTE TO PASTORS' WIVES:

No other women in the world are due such honor and respect as faithful pastors' wives. Unless you have served the Lord in that role and calling, you cannot fully understand, though you observe these remarkable ladies continually.

I can remember my own ignorance before I became a pastor's wife; before the Lord called my husband to preach and later to his own pastorate where he served forty-two years.

After nearly thirty of those years in the pastorate, I began writing a book about our ministry from the beginning. It turned out to be more work than I had remotely imagined, so the unfinished project wound up stuffed in the back of my file and soon forgotten. I was reminded of it recently and decided to quote from the first chapter which describes the beginning for me in the role of the pastor's wife. I was a layman's wife in our home church in Grand Prairie, TX in the late 1950's.

Excerpt from: *Between The Lines* by Edna Holmes.

"Our home church had hosted the monthly fellowship meeting for pastors. Many of their wives also attended. Our pastor's wife arranged a special session for them so they could share ideas and demonstrate teaching helps and techniques.

"Our church women were allowed to come in too, and I felt so privileged to have an opportunity to be near and observe these special ladies. In my estimation, pastors' wives were next to angels, and each one represented an interesting story I'd love to read. Before realizing what I was doing, I blurted out "I wish I were a pastor's wife! After an awkward moment of silence, the meeting continued.

"That was over fifty years ago, but I remember the reaction of those pastors' wives to my impulsive outburst. They just looked at me...thoughtfully. Now, I understand what they knew that day."

The things involved in the work of the ministry are not generally known or understood by those outside of it. The working of the Lord which molds a wife into an effective help-meet for her husband in the ministry, in a pastorate, is not visible on the surface, but hidden 'between the lines' of her life.

Little did I realize the wish would come true, for within months God did call my husband to be a preacher. A few years afterwards, he became the pastor of a little church in a country town. It pleased the Lord to keep us in that same pastorate for forty-two years. In the fall of 1962, I moved into a little parsonage behind Bethel Baptist Church in Grapevine, TX and straightway tumbled *between the lines* where I began to learn by endless experience what makes pastors' wives look thoughtful.

The situations thrust into the life of a pastor's wife may be unique because of the nature of her role in the ministry; but the knowledge she acquires by experience is common to the needs of all Christian women. Many pastors' wives are effective teachers and spiritual advisors for the women in their churches. The things of the Lord effecting our spiritual growth, through various trials and learning experiences, are not always seen with our eyes...only the results, as He patiently guides us toward maturity. *Job 23:14 "For he performeth the thing that is appointed for me: and many such things are with him."*

The wonder of it all and how God accomplishes this in His children cannot be fully explained; and for the most part, it remains concealed *between the lines* of the life of those in ministry, and all Christians.

A PREACHER'S WIFE

She is marked and designated
Like a package stamped with 'fragile',
And for her peculiar station in life,
She must needs be spiritually agile.

No creature having two distinct heads
Gets more careful observation
Than the wife of a godly preacher;
She's a prize in God's creation.

That lady secures much comfort
For her husband of the cloth,
Plus her children and countless others:
Home and church, lady of both.

As the saints march in and out
Of church at Sunday's worshipping,
She's there and cheerful, no matter what,
Perfecting the image she's keeping.

Sometimes between the doleful hours
Of midnight and six AM
She may actually come 'unglued',
Certain not to be heard...or seen.

Her husband may be understanding
And loving and kind as can be.
That really helps, but most of all,
The Lord's strength is what she needs.

It's a peculiar calling that's on her
Throughout this earthly life.
If she's ever been, she'll forever be
Known as 'A Preacher's Wife'.

EDNA HOLMES

The Child Poems

INTRODUCTION TO THE CHILD POEMS

A child sees his parents as his world, his frame of reference, his security and providers of all his needs. The only thing that can shake that world and disturb a little child is trouble between his parents whom he relies on for everything in his life.

My parents' marital problems were mild compared to what many families experience, but they did separate for a brief period of time when they were younger and it made a lasting impression on me. Because being away from my father and siblings, and attending a different school at seven years of age was very disconcerting, and the unkind treatment of other, older children added to my misery of heart and mind.

Nevertheless, decades later, that experience would prove to be an asset to our ministry in the pastorate. I've been able to counsel with children, with a similar, or much worse, background of childhood trauma. A child *knows if you really know* how he feels, and that only comes if you have experienced it.

The Child poems were *born* because they had to be. Since they have been out, some people have been ministered to by the simple, though poignant message they hold.

A PLAINTIVE LITTLE SONG

Once there was a Child
Who was wounded by those she loved.
She ran far away...and hid.
In time, she timidly came out to discover
That her world had grown old...
Bravely, she sang a plaintive little song;
Then, content, she quietly went away.

CHOOSE

"Choose." They said.

The Child, numb with disbelief,
sat in silence.

"Choose one of us!" They urged,

Each with a note of confidence,

Waiting for her to speak.

Desperately hoping, she murmured

"Both of you..."

A decision was made.

The child slipped away from the scene,

Clutching a treasure in her tattered heart.

I did not choose...

I did not choose.

SEPARATION

One scraggly flower bush marked the yard

Surrounding the house down the road

Suitable for separation.

The Child dug bare toes in the sand,
and pondered the thing.

Gloom hovered in the house, and the
yard was lonely.

She heard, then saw the car drawing near
the bend in the road.

Gladness sprang up as she recognized
that familiar face,

Near...yet so far away.

Motionless, she watched, vaguely hoping.

He drove past...a stranger.

Reluctantly, the Child tucked it away

In her heart...already heavy with reality.

Separation.

ALONGSIDE

She walked along scuffing bare

Feet through the sand,

Awed by the vastness of the blue sky,

And her desperate feeling of aloneness.

Life was broken down like

A dilapidated fence which

Secures no boundary or protection.

Could she have seen her *Protector* that day!

Near, watching, loving, molding,

Fashioning that little lump;

He was ageless...

She was seven.

RED RUBBER BOOTS

In the days between shoes and barefooted,
The last schooldays of May,
With the weather growing much warmer;
The Child walked alone each day.

It was during the separation...
With no one in which to confide
The problem of the red rubber boots
She wore daily; that's all she had.

Designed for water, snow and ice,
Nobody was now wearing the like.
They laughed and teased as children do.
The Child longed to run away and hide.

Pressed beyond measure to action,
She thought of a way she could do,
And diligently sought a puddle each day
To wade her red rubber boots through.

On the days she found one, how thrilling
To arrive with messed up boots!
The lot of her tormentors at school
Were so impressed...they were mute.

The Child learned from that experience,
Shut up in despairing days too;
You can cope with whatever you've got;
Look for a puddle...wade on through.

ON BEING INSECURE

*Like a little four year old blind girl in the
middle of a forty acre field....*

The distinguished speaker had said.

Memory raced back through the years;

Life had crumbled bit by bit.

Desperate, the Child stumbled blindly through

The rubble...searching for something,

Something to cling to.

Turning from the emptiness of the future,

Her groping heart uncovered

A pleasant memory of the past.

The Child curled herself around it...

And rested.

EARLY MEMORY

She crept nearer the conversation,
Unnoticed, as they discussed...returning.

Their faces towered above her,
But the Child studied them for hope.

Then she sought the hillside near the house
Where, ironically, the bitter-weeds

Grew in profusion; their dull yellow faces
stared curiously.

She grieved inwardly for her broken world...
Never to be the same again,

And gazed in wonder at her future
Suspended over an ocean of emptiness.

Mercifully, *One* drew the curtain
Of her memory and stored it away

In His time...and eternal purpose.

Note: Once a young child has had his life traumatically disturbed by the marital conflict of his parents, he grows up with a keen sense of awareness of *silent suffering* going on in little children in a similar situation. Fear and despair cannot be concealed in the eyes and on the faces of children. They haven't learned the art of *wearing a mask* as adults readily do to hide their true feelings.

SIMILE

Helpless...his youthful face

Pictured locked-in despair,

As he sat huddled in the back seat of the car,

While his parents stabbed one another

With double-meaning words.

But the child knew...

My heart melted into his, and we throbbed

Together for a moment of agony...

And then they drove away.

TO REMEMBER

Angry words flew between us

Driving home that night.

The reason...unimportant then, as now.

The little hand reached from the back

And patted my shoulder soothingly,

Pleading...

My heart retreated quickly from the conflict,

Remembering, almost too late.

Little son, I know...*I know.*

Note: The Child, in adulthood, is usually insecure and may have difficulty venturing out into the mainstream of society without fear and trepidation.

PETALS

With bulging pockets, the child
Approached the familiar place.
Quietly, she filled her hand with petals,
Then flung them from tiptoes over the wall.

They floated down onto the path of those
Whose clamor of life-sounds drifted
Faintly through the stony curtain.
The child snuggled against the wall
Straining to hear...scarcely breathing.

"What lovely petals...and such sweet fragrance.
Where did they come from?...I've never
Seen anything so beautiful..."

Smiling with satisfaction, the child pressed her back
To the stones warmed now by the sun.
She dug stray petals from her pockets,
And pressed them to her cheeks
Savoring the sweet odor.

Then, sighing, she retraced her steps
Back over the worn path
Marked by the softly curling petals
Fallen along the way.

SANDS OF TIME

Someone else was suffering;
I didn't know...could not see,
Being numbed by life's uncertainty;
I was senseless to others' needs.

Days, months, and years of time
Made decades of my life,
Filled with silent anguish
Words somehow can't describe.

Then one day...mercifully,
Knowing not why or how;
An ebbing flow of healing balm
Began and is in me now.

It has washed away some debris,
And that awful sense of loss.
I see precious things protruding
In the sands of time I'll cross.

I'm treading now with lighter steps
My valleys and lofty peaks.
Far behind me in the distance
Are broken shackles in a heap.

THOUGHT TO PONDER

"The past beckons; but betrays those
Who wander back into its vast emptiness,
Searching for treasured moments,
Following an emotional cord to its frayed end."

Psalm 28:7 "The Lord is my strength and my shield; my heart trusted in him, and I am helped: therefore my heart greatly rejoiceth; and with my song will I praise him."

A HAPPY LITTLE SONG

It was a happy little song
Buried deep in me.
It struggled in a mournful frame
For expression...to be free.

But plowing in life's soil was deep,
There was no place for a song.
Ceaseless toil in planting time
Made a quietness in my soul.

Then one day tender plants appeared:
New things began to grow.
The little song burst out of its bonds,
Startling my very soul.

I'd feared to sing it for sadness;
The years kept it muted for me.
Now that little song fills my days,
Singing what I can be...to me.

Grandma Bit

EDNA HOLMES

Grandmothers are privileged mothers who have raised their children, and lived to see their children's children come on the scene. They can enjoy this new generation, love them, spoil them in a nice way, make loads of good memories for them and yet they are not responsible, in normal situations, for rearing them. Life is as good as it can get for privileged grandmas.

There are many *pet* names grandchildren may call their grandmothers. All five of my grandchildren call me 'Grandma'. Through the years I've written some little personal poems for their birthdays. I've helped little hands make countless batches of cookies, read to them, and enjoyed many *nights at Grandma's* where I'd give manicures, brush long hair, and generally enjoy my precious grandchildren. All too soon, they are grown, in college or already graduated and pursuing their own lives. I'm not through making memories though. I learned how to *text* just so I can communicate with my grandchildren. *"I love you"* goes well any way you send it!

Grandmothers, I urge you to use your *grand* title with all its privileges and enjoy the time you have with your grandchildren. Use opportunities for showing them the love of God in your life, lift them up daily to the Lord in prayer, and share the Word of God with them on their level when they are small children. Write special things about your grandchildren and give them as part of their birthday gifts. It doesn't have to be *professional* type writing; it will be something special from your heart on paper that they can keep and treasure. I've written little personal poems and stories for them in their childhood days. It's just *grandma* stuff that let them know how special they are to us, their grandparents.

Call me a *doting* grandma. It's a lovely title.

ERIC

He is the very first grandson
On all sides of the family;
Quite a spot to fill up,
But he takes to it very kindly.

He knows he's got most everything
A boy could want or need;
His Dad and Mom and sisters
Make his happy home complete.

Besides all that and friends,
There's doting grandparents too,
Who think their grandson, Eric,
Is wonderful through and through.

He's got the wheel of success lined up
With home, church, and school; he's bold.
Look out world, take notice...
Today, Eric's eleven years old!

ERIN LEANNE

Life has snatched you forward so quickly,
I turned back to reminisce, to gaze for signs,
Though none can capture youth and hold it
From its destiny of kind.

Your youthful steps were sometimes faltering;
But grew steady in a determined frame.
Those steps are vivid in memory's recall,
And my heart feels a tug...remembering.

Then growing steps danced all around us
And somehow settled into a graceful mode.
They skipped through years like rows of flowers
That bloom a season, and then are gone.

Your steps have graced our lives and others;
A treasure we'll keep through all life's scenes.
Now they lead on toward maturity,
And destiny beckons...you're eighteen!

MICHELLE'S DAY

In-between 'little girl' and 'big girl'
In a mixture of baffling things;
Ideas not set in a permanent mold,
But entertaining just the same.

What to be when one grows up?
Well, something nobody's ever been.
It going to be really, really neat:
A profession folks have never seen.

There is no limit, secured as I am,
With ties to my family;
And faith in God which lets me see
The upward direction designed for me.

This teenage road is kind of rough;
I'll walk carefully in this scene.
Someday, I'll look back and smile,
Remembering when I was only fourteen.

THE FIRST YEAR

I arrived in unique fashion
Causing quite a stir in the place.
My Dad and Mom were overjoyed
To finally see my sweet face.
Little songs were learned quickly
Because Mommy insisted on singing
As she changed diapers, gave my bath,
Fed me, or just when hugging.

I squeezed into my Daddy's heart,
And wrapped Mommy around my finger.
My grandparents doted on my care;
Life to me couldn't be kinder.
Learning to sit up all alone,
My eyes could see all the sights.
Our house is full of tempting stuff;
I giggled a lot from delight.

The day came...I was crawling,
Plundering like a little bear,
But discovered to my great surprise
That "No! No!" time was here!
My little fat hand was spatted
For each discovery I made;
I finally tried for culture,
And unwound Daddy's Beethoven tape...

I'm walking now, how thrilling:
Holding little fists full of air;
Stretching my arms' length excitedly
To reach whatever's out there
This year's been very special,
Especially for Dad and Mommy.
They've learned how to be good parents
All because of Michael...that's ME!

CRYSTAL

Nineteen is a small heap of years, but in them
You have grown into a young lady with character,
A rare treasure in this generation of youth.

You've *actually* listened and communicated
With a loving father and mother
Which is outdated and old-fashioned etc.
But so valuable to well-being and development.

We won't dwell on beauty here...
You hear too much of that (perhaps)
But you are gifted that way...*bonito...bonito.*

However, it's your personal faith in God
And good character that will enrich your life.
Out of that flows trust-worthiness,
Kindness and lady-like qualities that affect
Everyone you meet in life.

You are moving gracefully from childhood
And youth, into the realm of adulthood.
Nothing is lost of the precious past...
Your grandparents have enough pictures
To chronicle all your life!

As you move on little girl, we will always
Be your best cheering section
And admiration society.
Happy Birthday!

Our daughter, Jeanne, at five years old, was the flower girl in my brother's wedding. In a picture taken of her with the bride, she looks exactly like her own daughter, when Crystal was that age.

FLOWER GIRL
(Crystal's View)

In the wedding picture one can see
A little girl that looks like me.
Shy and smiling, she is so pretty
In the glow of the bride's lovely gown.

Along the aisle she dropped flower petals,
Fragrant and vivid with color,
Then posed and looked right at me;
The flower girl is my mother!

Note: Taken from the poem THREE LOOKS elsewhere in this book, the last verse quoted here describes our daughter as the beautiful bride she was at her wedding thirty one years ago.

"She came down the aisle that day at last,
A vision in white satin ruffles and lace.
Filmy illusion fell from snowy brim
Veiling the bride's radiant smiling face.
It was that once in a lifetime scene
For the groom, looking steadfastly at his bride.
He guided her gently to their place to vow.
We observed the wonder...the look in his eyes,
But lack fitting words that *look* to describe."

Note: Recently Crystal was married to her fiancé, Scott Kolb. We attended that lovely wedding where her Grandfather was honored to perform the marriage ceremony. He has done that for all three of our granddaughters, now married.

At the rehearsal luncheon the day before the wedding, Scott's mother told a charming story about her son just past his toddler age. With permission I've used that story and written a little poem. It was a poignant moment when Mrs. Kolb presented the little rings she had kept for nineteen years to our granddaughter, Crystal.

GIVE THESE TO MY WIFE

The day had come to relinquish the treasure
To the girl she loved as a daughter;
Whose sparkling diamond on her hand
Enhanced the value of the two little bands.

Could she ever forget that long ago day
When her little son was pursuing his play?
She came to watch him work his toys
And noticed one hand in a fist tightly closed.

On inquiry of what he held in his hand,
He opened to show two colorful bands.
They changed to priceless before her eyes
As he spoke with clarity: *"Give these to my wife"*

Startled at the thought from her little boy's mind,
She took the little rings to a safe place to keep;
Waiting and wondering through years of time
Until this day, the promise to complete.

With motherly pride and tearful happiness,
She presented the rings to his lovely bride.
The memory would remain all of her life:
Her little son's directive: *"Give these to my wife!"*

LOVE...

I cannot describe love...Love describes me.

Quietly it came; so subtle I was not aware
Until my days were filled with thoughts of him;
It was his voice in the crowd I listened to hear.

Persistent in expression,
Love would not be concealed: in the eyes,
Tone of voice and my guarded sighs...

Then one day what did I see?
At a glance in his eyes, I saw love
Looking back at me.

Today our lives blend together,
Sparked by love, sealed with commitment
To God...and each other.

I cannot describe love...
Rather, love describes me,
And those who love.

Note: The poem, LOVE, on the previous page, was written for our granddaughter, Erin, and read at her wedding to Shane Jacobus in March of 2007.

The following poem ODE TO COURTSHIP was written for our granddaughter, Michelle, and was read at her wedding to Karl Herb in October 2012.

ODE TO COURTSHIP

A wedding is beautiful and solemn; sacred things are.
But the courtship that caused this lovely event
Sparkles with accumulated memories
That will bring smiles and laughter
Long after the honeymoon is past
And life is ordinary but satisfying in marriage.

Actually, he first noticed her car,
A 'hand me down' from Grandpa:
A cumbersome Buick that had to be skillfully
Maneuvered to fit any parking space.
Evidently, she'd managed; he admired that.

His opportunity came one evening, when she sat down
To chat with neighbors after walking her dog.
After that initial meeting, he knew she had a quiet
Disposition, was somewhat guarded,
And had great affection for her pet.
He made a very important decision that night.
I'll have to make friends with that dog...

She was *not* going to be distracted by that good looking
Guy downstairs; she intended to stay focused.
However, he had made friends with her dog.

On a 'just friends' date, she discovered
Qualities she admired...a gentle heart,
Honesty and other appealing things.
Her attraction for him grew and blossomed
Into love, that changed her life.

Their love has brought us together to share this moment
And hear their vows. They have wisely chosen
To acknowledge God, to worship Him and follow
His guidance in their future.
Such love, such wisdom, will never fail.

Note: We were blessed to have our first great-grandchild born in September of 2011. Jovie Beulah Jacobus. I was motivated to write the following little poem when I saw the many sonogram pictures of Jovie on display before that little girl was born!

BABY'S THOUGHTS

In my little nook of creation,
There's only God and me...to be.
From the miracle of my beginning He is
'Fearfully and wonderfully' making me.

I'm perfect already, yet unfinished,
And not ready for inspection's glare;
But suddenly, without warning to me,
Light probed the darkness of mystery here.

What's Mommy and Daddy eager to see,
My fingers and toes, and if it's really me?
When God completes my every part,
I'll move to their arms and loving hearts.

Now in the last curious light of detection
My heart was shown beating to perfection
To assure those eagerly awaiting me,
I'm nearly done...soon you will see.

Note: The first big event for Jovie was serving as the flower girl in her Aunt Michelle's wedding. She was one year old. Jovie will not remember that time, but she was a charming part of the wedding.

THE LITTLEST FLOWER GIRL

That's what I was supposed to do,
Go down the aisle between massive pews.
I left my handprints on the ends...
It shows that's where I've been.

I walked down right before the bride;
My Daddy's strong hand held to mine.
I smiled and charmed with big blue eyes;
There were teary smiles and sighs...

Then I saw Momma at the end
Dressed so pretty awaiting the bride.
Daddy swooped me away then,
But I saw a tear sparkling in her eye.

I won't remember that wedding day,
Solemn and happy with things in a whirl.
But our family history holds it all:
I was the Littlest Flower Girl!

Note: Each year we have received a calendar from our grandchildren featuring Jovie's picture each month. I was inspired to try and *capture* some of her pretty expressions in little poems. I consider these things *handprints* so our great grandchildren will know that we have been in their lives when they grow up and we are long gone from the scene.

PEEK-A-BOO

Peek-a-boo! I see you;
Her blue eyes sparkled merrily.
It was a game as I could see,
Her watching every move by me.

Behind the cabinet and cabinet doors
I'd look suddenly to surprise.
But all I saw was amusement
Dancing in those big blue eyes.

Days of April's spring were spent,
Fast as slow goes for a Great-Ma
Playing peek-a-boo with Jovie blue eyes,
Watching from the calendar on the wall.

CALENDAR GIRL

In the prettiest pose you'll ever see
Is our calendar girl that's nearly three.
Standing with poise, she is little-girl tall,
Straight as an arrow shot from a bow.

Happiness shows on our littlest girl,
With merriment sparkling in her blue eyes.
Secure and loved, she has only 'to be'
As the calendar turns, and she will be three!

Note: Now Jovie will be *sharing the hugs* and she is delighted! Her baby brother, Zed Miller Jacobus, was born this year in July. She is the happiest big sister and that sturdy little boy has already taken his place in that happy family.

AS YOU SEE

Jovie's getting a hug...as you see,

Because I'm Momma's favorite'

For hugging, except for Poppa;

He was here before me.

And I'm thinking...as you see.

There's more to ponder when you're three.

With memories budding; it's fun for me;

But inside the hugs, I'm happiest to be.

Note: I made each of my granddaughters a *heart* quilt when they were young. Consisting of twelve inch blocks with a big heart appliquéd in each one, they were very pretty. The girls have kept them. Now Erin's *heart* quilt is on Jovie's bed. She had me to put a new binding on the edges, and at that time, I added a little pocket *full of hugs* on one of the hearts to make the quilt special for Jovie.

We should make the days we have with grandchildren and then *great grandchildren* count as though they will remember every minute of the time. More than likely, *they will remember!*

I've seen little children and adults alike, at funerals, grieving the passing of their grandparents. If we sow love and attention in our grandchildren and great grandchildren that is the way it will be.

ABOUT THE AUTHOR

Edna Holmes grew up, a country girl, the third one of ten children. The rich and varied experiences of her childhood are often referenced in her writing.

She married her *soldier home from the war* at an early age and five years later they both became Christians through a personal faith in Jesus Christ. Their focus changed immediately. Years later her husband became the pastor of a church in Grapevine, TX. He would serve faithfully in that pastorate for forty-two years.

Within those decades the church grew to be strong in their missions outreach: contributing to the support of many missionary families serving all over the world. Edna was privileged to travel with her husband to many countries as he visited the missionaries, encouraging them in their work. She learned from experience that Christian women all over the world, in all cultures, have the same basic needs and desires of the heart.

During those years Edna began writing poems, with the first being a collection of *Memories in Verse* about her childhood days with her family on the farm. Growing up in a large family of ten children in the country, in the era before electricity, running water, and telephones, gives one the richest of resources to draw on in writing.

Part I of this book consists of that collection. Other poems and writings in other categories make up Part II.

Edna and her husband, Louis, are enjoying their older years as they continue to serve the Lord in speaking, encouraging young pastors and their wives in the ministry, and generally being of help where they are needed. Their chief joy otherwise is their family: children, grandchildren, and great-grandchildren.

Edna's first published book, *Treasures To Keep*, contains 365 Daily Devotionals and is currently available at www.amazon.com, in both paperback and Kindle editions.

Note: Several other of my siblings are also authors. To see their publications go to www.amazon.com and search for their names:

Willie Holt
Dan Holt
John Holt
Max Holt
Connie Hall

www.ingramcontent.com/pod-product-compliance
Lightning Source LLC
Chambersburg PA
CBHW060038040426
42331CB00032B/1006